BLACK IMAGES
IN THE COMICS

A VISUAL HISTORY

by Fredrik Strömberg

BLACK IMAGES IN THE COMICS

A VISUAL HISTORY

by Fredrik Strömberg

with a foreword by Charles Johnson

FANTAGRAPHICS BOOKS

BLACK IMAGES IN THE COMICS
A VISUAL HISTORY

© 2003 Fredrik Strömberg and Fantagraphics Books.
Foreword © 2003 Charles Johnson.
Editor: Kim Thompson.
Copy editor, American edition (pp. 1-103), and
author, pages 65, 69, 71, 89 and 205: David Gerstein.
Author, pages 51 and 161: Bennie Bødker.
Graphic design: Fredrik Strömberg. Cover design: Tony Ong.
Proofreading (Swedish edition): Peter Nilsson.
Proofreading (2012 U.S. edition): Janice Lee.
Associate Editor: Eric Reynolds.
Published by: Gary Groth and Kim Thompson.

I would also like to thank the following persons:
Michael Barrier, Robert L. Beerbohm, Geoffrey Blum, Mark
Evanier, Håkan Fredriksson, Stefano Gaudiano, Joakim Gunnarsson,
Jakob Hallin, Jostein Hansen, Michel Kempeneers, Christian
Kindblad, Pascal Lefèvre, Freddy Milton, Stig Pilgaard-Olsen,
Claes Reimerthi, Eric Reynolds, Don Rosa, Peter Sattler, John
Wells, Lina Willman, E. Zeiger – and all the others who
helped in my search for information and graphics.

First softcover printing: May 2012.

ISBN 978-1-60699-562-4   Printed in China

FOREWORD
BY DR. CHARLES JOHNSON

Dere ain't no room on dis Earth fo' dem white boys an' me.
                    Sambo and His Funny Noises, 1914.

What, if anything, does 200 years of cartoon images depicting Black people tell us about ourselves?

This question, very troubling, was foremost in my thoughts as I turned the pages of Fredrik Strömberg's *Black Images in the Comics*, the professional cartoonist in me fascinated – both appalled and intrigued – by this book's cornucopia of culturally sedimented images. His well-chosen selections provide a chronological survey of the comic strip's evolution from the antebellum period to the present, and this ambitious compilation is at times startling and original in its breadth, covering not merely the American and European contributions to comic art purporting to represent Black people, but works from Africa, Japan, and the United Arab Emirates as well. The author does, however, overlook certain American oddities like *All-Negro Comics* in 1947; Doris

McClarty's 1950s strip "Fireball Freddie" in *Hep*; Brumsic Brandon's syndicated strip *Luther,* and his daughter Barbara Brandon's Feiffer-esque feature *Where I'm Coming From*; and many publishers of independent Black comics in the 1990s such as Posro Komics' *MC Squared: A Man With a Serious Game Plan*, but this is a small quibble. On the whole, and in general, Strömberg's pop study is a sturdy example of dedication and research that deserves a place on our bookshelves beside Trina Robbins's essential *A Century of Women Cartoonists*, and not too far down the shelf from Harvard University Press' seminal, four-volume *The Image of the Black in Western Art*.

But while the cartoonist and comics scholar in me coolly and objectively appreciated the impressive archeology of images assembled in *Black Images in the Comics*, as a Black American reader my visceral reaction to this barrage of racist drawings from the 1840s through the 1940s was revulsion and a profound sadness.

How else could a Black person respond to a parade of generic, dancing silhouettes; savage, cannibalistic Africans; language-mangling Boskos; and bubble-lipped, buffoonish sidekicks like *The Spirit*'s "Ebony"? As the great, late Black cartoonist Ollie Harrington once put it, white illustrators invariably drew Negroes as "a circle, black with two hotdogs in the middle for a mouth." More importantly, the creators of this inhuman iconography – like Harriet Beecher Stowe in *Uncle Tom's Cabin* or D.W. Griffith's *Birth of a Nation* (aka *The Clansman*) – did not envision, as they sat penciling and inking into the wee hours of the morning at their drawing tables, Black Americans as their audience. We were not part of the artist/audience equation. These were products (as unreal as the ubiquitous imagery for today's Roswell aliens, the "Grays") that included supposedly Black characters but were composed *by* and *for* whites, and if these images can serve us at all in the twenty-first century, they are only useful as the transcript of a pre-World War II, WASP imagination completely unmoored from reality.

During this same period, of course, comic books and strips offered equally repulsive and fantastic portraits of avaricious Jewish immigrants. For example, one ancient cartoon entitled "He Saw Him First" portrayed three Jewish merchants, all with bulbous noses, one wearing a yarmulke, and offered this caption: *Einstein:* "Cohen caught a burglar in his shtore last night und turned him over to der police." *Isaacs:* "Vat a fool! Vhy didn't he rob him himself?" Clownish Irishmen appeared in "Saving His Strength," a panel in which two Irishmen sit drinking and smoking cigars. *Casey:* "Did ye go over t'see Kelly lasht night?" *Costigan:* "Oi did not. After Oi'd walked two-thirds av th' way Oi was too toired t'go a shtep further, so Oi turned round an' walked back home again." There were also Chinese with pigtails and nine-inch fingernails (See Atlas/Marvel Comics' 1952 series *Yellow Claw);* and buck-toothed, squinty-eyed Japanese (I refer the reader to *any* World War II propaganda-drenched comic book, such as *Young Allies* or *Captain America*). In other words, in American comic art we find risible yet demeaning (and often dangerous) images of *all* racial Others, which demands a separate study itself and is of enormous importance as American comic artists and editorial cartoonists today confront the serious question of how to portray the diversity among Muslims and people from the Middle East. But we must remember that since the European Age of Exploration, when whites first encountered and entered into sustained relations with Africans, the Negro has been the very special object of the white man's deepest – and perhaps primordial – fears and fantasies; he was seldom conceived as fully human, or culturally and intellectually equal, and was granted by whites superiority in but one area – the physical, i.e., he was placed, ontologically, on the same plane as the animals or brute matter, like the earliest depictions of Mandrake the Magician's hulking assistant "Lothar."

What I find most interesting – and chilling – about the pre-1950s images of Blacks in this volume is the stubborn, willful ignorance that comic artists from Winsor McCay to Walter Lantz displayed in terms of African and Black American history and culture (which *is* American history and culture since 1619 when the first 20 Black indentured servants arrived at the Jamestown colony). One can only conclude that these creators knew nothing – absolutely nothing – about their Black subjects. In his prologue, Strömberg says, "Comics are a medium of extremes. They often simplify and stereotype their subjects." He suggests that some apologists for the racist cartoon images of the past would argue that "cartoonists tend to represent people from other nationalities with stereotypical appearances simply because it is harder to give individual appearances to persons from a national group other than your own." If these images spring from an epistemological difficulty or a technical dilemma related to draftsmanship rather than purely racist intent ("I, no matter how much I try, never will be able to see the world from the point of view of a Black person," says Strömberg, unintentionally echoing D.H. Lawrence in his 1924 essay for

Vanity Fair, "On Being a Man," where he writes, "I am not a nigger and so I can't know a nigger, and I can never fully 'understand' him" – but that, of course, is the very *point* of art, comic or otherwise: to put us "over there" behind the eyes of Others), then we should call this visual short-hand for people of color by its proper name: intellectual and creative *laziness*.

Personally, as a Black cartoonist, I don't buy the idea that an artist is merely a creature of his time, a *tabula rasa* inscribed with the bigoted beliefs of his *Zeitgeist*. That, if you think about it, is no more than the flimsiest excuse for a lack of invention, daring, or innovation in one's compositions – the artist, in effect, is content to uncritically work with *received*, pre-fabricated imagery and ideas minted in the minds of others (like Joel Chandler Harris, the Plantation School writers and illustrators, or Margaret Mitchell's *Gone With the Wind*). When I was fifteen years old, and studied with the Jewish cartoonist/writer Lawrence

Lariar, who served as cartoon editor for *Parade* magazine and *The Best Cartoons of the Year* in the 1960s, one of his lessons – a chapter in the workbook he gave his students – was devoted precisely to the importance of avoiding stereotypes when drawing nonwhite characters and individuating them as fully as possible. (Thus, I cannot believe that Robert Crumb's grotesque and pornographic character "Angelfood McSpade" in the underground comics of the 1960s is avant-garde or provocative in any positive way.) The point, if I haven't made it clear already, is that when we turn the pages of *Black Images in the Comics*, we should remember that the pictures we are looking at, these Ur-images of Blacks, are a testament to the failure of the imagination (and often of empathy, too), and tell us nothing about Black people but *every*thing about what white audiences approved and felt comfortable with in pop culture until the 1950s when relentless agitation by the NAACP and Civil Rights workers finally made them unacceptable, hugely embarrassing for citizens of a democratic republic, and relegated them to the trash heap of human evolution. The effect of exposure to these images is not unlike what viewers experience at the end of Spike Lee's controversial film, *Bamboozled*, which presents a lengthy montage of surrealistic, ultimately mind-numbing images of Blacks in American films.

Are the cartoon images of Blacks *after* the 1950s an improvement? Strömberg concludes his book, and correctly, with this observation: "Blacks in comics are still sadly few, even if they – when they do appear – seem to be less stereotypical. Quite often the reader gets a feeling that a Black character is included just to be *the* Black character in a certain context. That people from different ethnic minorities are included without being representative of their whole group is still relatively unusual." (Well might we say the same about Blacks in the majority of Hollywood motion-pictures.) And he adds, "What is probably needed are more Black comics creators because of the simple fact… it is impossible to give a totally correct view of the life of someone else."

That "totally correct view" of the racial Other is no doubt not even desirable – comics have never aspired to being a mimetic art, and what, we must ask, is "correct" about white lives in strips like *Dick Tracy* or Johnny Hart's *B.C.*? No, Black people offer a surplus of meaning in lives too widely diversified for a single image or character to contain. If we look at the earliest syndicated comic strips by Black cartoonists in the 1960s and '70s – Morrie Turner's *Wee Pals* and Ted Shearer's *Quincy* – we see that their creators, influenced by the soaring rhetoric of Martin Luther King Jr., flew their work under the flag of integration, equality, and brotherhood. White cartoonists during that period did the same when they added Black characters to their *dramatis personae*. So far so good. But of these humorous, inoffensive comics we can say what an acquaintance of mine said about characters on *The Cosby Show* : "They're just like white people, only cuter."

Fortunately, other Black cartoonists later ventured into areas less cute, tackling dysteleological elements in inner-city Black life (Ray Billingsley's *Curtis*), offering edgy social commentary from an Afrocentric viewpoint (*The Boondocks*), or exploring the effects of racism and colonialism. Clearly, this is progress in the portrayal of Blacks since the 1940s – comics that, as transitional works, point to greater artistic possibilities. But I feel that even these more realistically written and drawn comics are still reactive, self-consciously fighting against "cartoon coon" images from the period of Jim Crow segregation, struggling to correct old, apartheid-era wrongs and not yet fully and creatively *free*. Like Strömberg, I sense that something important – the next Great Leap Forward – is still missing in this popular medium.

And what might that be? Well, try this:

I wait for the day when I can turn to the comics pages in my daily newspaper and find a Black panel cartoonist with the wildly *free* and idiosyncratic vision that Gary Larson brought to *The Far Side*, and John Deering sometimes delivers in *Strange Brew*. I want to see a Black protagonist who is a prodigy inventor like Alan Moore and Kevin Nowlan's wonderfully conceived (and drawn) "Jack B. Quick, Boy Inventor" in *Tomorrow Stories*; or, in animated films, an African-American "Jimmy Neutron, Boy Genius." I long – as an American, a cartoonist, and a writer – for the day when my countrymen will accept and broadly support stories about Black characters that are complex, original (not sepia clones of white characters like "Friday Foster" or "Powerman"), risk-taking, free of stereotypes, and *not* about race or victimization. Stories in which a character who just happens to be Black is the emblematic, archetypal figure in which we – *all* of us – invest our dreams, imaginings, and sense of adventure about the vast possibilities for what humans can be and do – just as we have done, or been culturally indoctrinated to do, with white characters ranging from Blondie to Charlie Brown, from Superman to Dilbert, from Popeye to Beetle Bailey. (Odd, isn't it, that no one ever asks the ethnicity of those characters? Is Captain America *really* Jewish like his creators Jack Kirby and Joe Simon? Is Blondie a Swede? Is Popeye Irish? Is Charlie Brown German, perhaps descended from one of the Katzenjammer Kids? And, as the old joke goes, Walt Disney's Pluto is a dog, but what the hell is Goofy? A dog crossed with human DNA? Sorry, I couldn't resist that.) That day of liberation and enlightenment for Black images in comics has yet to come, and has been a long time coming. But, like Adam Clayton Powell, I "keep the faith" that some day, for the sake of my children and future generations who love comic art, it will.

Dr. Charles Johnson
January, 2003

Dr. Charles Johnson, a 1998 MacArthur Fellow, received the National Book Award for his novel Middle Passage *in 1990, and was a 2002 recipient of the Academy Award for Literature from the American Academy of Arts and Letters. He has published three other novels (*Dreamer, Oxherding Tale, *and* Faith and the Good Thing*), as well as three story collections (*The Sorcerer's Apprentice, Oulcatcher, *and* Dr. King's Refrigerator: And Other Bedtime Stories*). His other books include* King: The Photobiography of Martin Luther King Jr. *(coauthored with Bob Adelman)*, Africans in America: America's Journey Through Slavery *(co-authored with Patricia Smith)*, Being and Race: Black Writing Since 1970, Black Men Speaking *(coedited with John McCluskey Jr.)*, Turning the Wheel: Essays on Buddhism and Writing, *and two books of drawings. A literary critic, screenwriter, philosopher, international lecturer and cartoonist with over 1,000 drawings published, he is the S. Wilson and Grace M. Pollock Endowed Professor of English at the University of Washington in Seattle. You may visit his author's website at* <u>www.oxherdingtale.co</u>.

PREFACE TO THE NEW EDITION

Maybe the costume is in bad taste.

t's been more than ten years since I wrote the first version of the book *Black Images in the Comics – A Visual History*. God, how did that happen… When the book was released in the U.S. it garnered a lot of acclaim and even received a nomination for an Eisner Award (it didn't win, but it was up against the first big book on Chris Ware, so I wasn't surprised).

When I went to the San Diego Comic Convention for the book release, I was also invited to give a talk about the book, something I gladly accepted, even though this was to be the first time I held a lecture in English for a larger audience. I wasn't sure what to expect, but when entering the hall where I was supposed to give the talk and realizing that it was big and chock full of people, many of whom were African-Americans and all eagerly anticipating what I had to say, I must admit that it was a bit daunting. When I found out that I had been put in the section for academic studies, and given an "opponent," a really big African-American walking around with a paperboard taking notes when I was speaking, I started sweating a bit. When I was finished and had been given my applause, my "opponent" walked up to the podium, looked sternly out over the crowd, and said: "If there's anyone here who thinks that a white guy should not have written such a book, you can leave now!" To this day, Professor William H. Foster III is a great friend of mine.

The story of this book got started when I held a lecture on the subject in Sweden and realized when researching that there was actually no really good book on Black people in comics. I put together all that I had gathered for my lecture, started arranging the examples in chronological order, and went back to my library, looking for more interesting comics, and before I knew it I had written a book. This was published in Sweden in 2001 and was soon followed by a Danish edition in 2003, with some added Danish examples. I sent the Swedish edition to Fantagraphics, with a few pages translated, and was surprised, delighted, and a bit intimidated when I got the message that it was to be published in English. I did much more thorough research this time around, expanded the English edition with almost 50 percent more pages in order to make sure that I covered as many angles as possible, and on the whole the book became much better.

As I stated earlier, the book got very good reviews, sold out within a few years, and has since been fetching astronomical sums at antique bookshops. Then, recently, in 2010, there was a French edition (*Images Noires*) with a lot of new examples, and we got the idea to do a new, expanded softcover edition of the English version, which is what you are now holding in your hands, with some of that French material. What has been added to this new and expanded edition are mainly new examples in the very end of the book, mostly French and Belgian from the 1980s and onward and of course other comics from the 21st century, i.e. since the book was written.

This new edition is to be released in conjunction with my new book *Jewish Images in the Comics – A Visual History*, which I am writing right now. If you enjoy this book, do look it up.

Fredrik Strömberg, Malmö, Sweden, November 2011

Negro. Black. Colored. African-American. When I started writing this book, one of the first problems to present itself was which words to employ when referring to the subjects of my story. Whether used in reference to a foreign nationality or a local minority, these words are loaded to the point that they cannot be used without carrying certain connotations. But that happens to be my goal in the present volume: to study the manner in which Black (the term I finally, after a lot of agonizing, chose) people have, over the years, been portrayed in the world of comics – and to address the implications and larger issues that these portrayals raise. I am of course aware of the prejudiced associations many of these images carry, but that is exactly why it is important to confront them. I believe that it is only by admitting to, examining, and exposing the racism of yesterday that we can expose and oppose the racism of today.

The premise of this book is that the people who make comics have never existed in a vacuum. They instead live within a surrounding culture, a culture that is naturally reflected in their work. By studying the images that comics depict, we may thus acquire – both directly and indirectly – a snapshot of the realities in which the comics' creators lived. Our task is further facilitated by the fact that comics are a medium of extremes. They often simplify and stereotype their subjects, partly in an attempt to make our complex world understandable, partly as a means of efficient short-form communication. In the process, of course, they also highlight their surrounding societies' trends and attitudes, making them easily available for observation and study. Pop culture in general, and comics especially, can often do better than serious works of art in providing the researcher with a clear picture of the spirit of a certain time.

There are those who believe that cartoonists depict people from other ethnic and racial groups with stereotypical traits simply because it is harder to differentiate between persons from a national group other than one's own. According to this theory, the representations of certain minorities with clear iconic attributes simply reflects the fact that the artist has taken a shortcut, and does not necessarily betray genuine racism on the part of the individual cartoonist. If we accept this as true, then it becomes, if anything, even more interesting to examine what society has deemed acceptable at a certain point in time.

Racism in comics is not only a matter of the drawings, however. It can – as I see it – be distinguished on at least three levels: the first is the purely pictorial (in which a certain minority is depicted with various stereotypical attributes); the second is the purely textual (in which captions and not least the use of language present persons in a negative way); the third, and probably the most subversive, is on a content level (in which, for example, people from a certain minority are constantly portrayed as evil, stupid, foolish, subservient... or quite simply nonexistent).

This book is not a tightly-reasoned and impeccably-documented doctor's thesis on the subject of "the treatment of Black people in comics," but rather a personal reflection on what I have found in my comics collection (which is extensive, true, but in no way all-encompassing), and tips I have gotten from other comics historians and people interested in comics. *If* this had been a more academic text it would probably have been proper at this stage to introduce more theoretical definitions of terms such as "racism" and "prejudices." I could cite opinionmakers such as Peter Abélard (who claimed that the color of the skins of people from Africa was a sign of sin), de Gubineau (whose theories about the origin of the Aryans gave birth to the racial doctrine of the Nazis), and so on... but that is not really the aim of this book. Comics may be – as I wrote earlier – a mirror of society, which clearly makes it fruitful to apply to this medium the theories that were developed to explain other phenomena in that same society. The very premise of this book, though, is desire; the desire to write about an interesting phenomenon, which is why I want to steer clear of excessive theorizing.

In a way this book is going to be somewhat academic, because, no matter how much I try, I will never be able to see the world from the point of view of a Black person. Considering that – so far as I know – there still is no really good book on this subject, not even in the United States, it might be useful for a writer to view this phenomenon "from the outside"; although it is at least true that from a Swedish perspective – given that we are a small comics nation situated in the no-man's-land between two major comics cultures – it might be a bit easier to gain an overview, compared to writers based in either the Anglo-Saxon or the Franco-Belgian culture, who tend to overlook anything from "the outside."

Anyway, back to the disposition of this book. I hesitated between presenting my examples grouped thematically or chronologically. After a while it became clear to me that the latter was preferable, since it made the different stages that the representations of Blacks in comics have gone through more readily apparent. This means that I have presented everything in chronological order, and travel from the beginning of the 19th century – when Black characters first began appearing in comics – until today. I'll get back to this in the "Epilogue," – where I reflect upon the trends I have been able to discern in the material presented.

The chronological approach also prompted me, while I was working on this book, to present some more general facts about the development of comics to give the reader an overview of the history of the medium during this period. I would like to make a few comments on the specific history of comics before we start, however. Comics, depending on how you define the term, have a long and clouded past, originating in the ancient tradition of telling stories with pictures. The so-called "modern comics" were created in the United States in the late 1890s, and were mainly published in daily, weekly, and monthly periodicals aimed at adult readers. It was not until comics were being created directly for comics magazines that their aim shifted to a younger audience. This trend started in the United States in the 1930s and soon spread to the rest of the Western world. Comics aimed at children and young adults have dominated the market ever since then. During the 1960s a counterreaction occurred, which is arguably still in progress. It meant that cartoonists once again were doing comics for adult readers, a trend that has become even more pronounced in the last two decades or so. These very schematic stages can be useful to keep in mind when thinking about how Blacks have been treated in comics – since the intended audience naturally affects the cartoonist's ability to express him- or herself.

Another thing that should be mentioned before getting to the main part of the book is the variety of Black stereotypes that have evolved in popular culture, above all in the United States. These stereotypes do occur less frequently today, but they are so well established that their impact still can be seen in the most diverse contexts.

One can isolate at least seven different basic Black stereotypes that have been established in stories mostly aimed at a white public. I might call the first stereotype simply – for want of a better word – the **native**, namely the unflattering portrayal of native aborigines as childish savages both silly and dangerous. Next comes the **tom**, an eternally servile, humble, and forgiving soul who never questions the superiority of the white ruling class; his name derives from the traditional, if somewhat inaccurate, popular reading of Harriet Beecher Stowe's title character in *Uncle Tom's Cabin*. The third stereotype is the **coon** – a roguish, comedic figure known for his mischievous pranks and idiosyncratic approach to the English language; the fourth stereotype is the **piccaninny** – a younger version of the coon, prone to leaps of the imagination and "funny" bursts of overenthusiasm. The fifth type is the **tragic mulatto**, particularly common as a topic in films – a person (most often female) sexually torn between Black and white worlds, her sensual nature making her an "acceptable" object for white desire even as her Black legacy dooms her to tragedy. The sixth common stereotype is the **mammy**, a sort of feminine tom – complete with large, ungainly, asexual physique and an unwavering loyalty to the white household for which she works. The seventh and final stereotype, the **buck**, is a strong, violent and rebellious "bad Negro" – most often functioning as a cautionary example. I will return to these stereotypes, and discuss certain comics characters' relationships to them, later in this book.

I would also like to mention that the selection of comics from which I have chosen has been mostly limited to comics from the Western world, that is to say Europe and America, since the majority of the comics that are available in Sweden originates from these parts. That America, where approximately 12 percent of the inhabitants are Black, dominates in the selection should not come as a surprise. Neither should the fact that the comics from my own country, Sweden, might be a bit overrepresented considering the relatively small role Sweden has played in the history of comics... Sporadic excursions from these geographic areas *do* occur but I did – as I have already mentioned – not set out to create a definite academic thesis, and I am sure that important comic strips in the context have been neglected. People from Africa are, for example, often presented as subjects in comics, but African comics are much more unusual.

It would probably also have been interesting to examine how white people have been treated in comics in countries where the population is mainly Black. That, though, would be an entirely different book. If it had been an academic text I wanted to write, it would probably have been better to focus on one part of the world, or better yet one country, in order to point out connections and draw conclusions. It would, however, not have been as much fun – which is why this alternative never really was an alternative.

When reading this book you will probably think of several Black characters who "should" have been included, but my decision to cover Black images in comics from the whole world necessitated a certain winnowing down. For every image included in the book I have therefore discarded hundreds. The final selection was based on several criteria, such as the comic's importance in the history of the medium (since, on one level, I also wanted the book to give an overview of how comics have developed), the relative prominence of the Black characters in the story, whether the subject of racism was touched upon, or sometimes simply the fact that I found an image I couldn't resist...

One limitation I gave myself from the start was that each comic would be written about only once, and only for as long as is possible within a single page. This worked out fine for the most part, and hopefully helps highlight, for both me and the readers, the historical undercurrents that affected the cartoonists. In some cases a comic has existed for several decades and changed with time, which might make it worth examining more than once. (It would, for example, be interesting to look more closely at how Black people have been treated in *The Phantom*, which has gone through several different stages in the ca. 70 years of its existence.) But this would also have led to a different book than the one I wanted to write. I, quite simply, have chosen not to write about a certain comic more than once, because I wanted to include as many different comics as possible without creating too unwieldy a book.

I should probably also mention that I have chosen to examine images only from comics, and that my definition of comics is "juxtaposed pictures in deliberate sequence." This disqualifies cartoons, illustrations for magazines, and many other drawn pictures that probably would have been very interesting to examine. I have done this partly to make my search manageable, and partly because I am interested in the narrative quality that exists within comics, but is more or less lacking in discrete pictures.

The more orderly reader might, at this point, object to the fact that I have chosen to illustrate my book with separate, single images – in a way, "out of sequence." This choice is based not solely on aesthetics, to make sure that each panel could be reproduced at a satisfying size, but also because I from the very beginning had a vision of a book just like the one you are now holding in your hand.

BLACK
IMAGES

When Slaves are purchased they are generally marked on the breast with a red hot Iron.

will begin my visual history with a panel from an unsigned, so-called "documentary atrocity strip" created in England at the beginning of the 19th century. Many comics historians are convinced that this is a period in which the comic strip as such did not even exist. Many old-school American scholars still consider the form to have originated in the United States some ninety years later. The image to the left, however, is part of a narrative told in a clear sequence of pictures with added texts – which according to my definition makes it a comic. At the start of the 1800s there were major campaigns to end slavery in Britain, resulting finally in its abolition in the colonies in 1834. Both before and after this, comics – then distributed as individual printed pages – tackled this hot topic. Cartoonists often took the side of the slaves and showed the reader the atrocities inflicted upon them. This particular example, "**Remarks on the Methods of procuring slaves, with a short Account of their Treatment in the West Indies,**" shows in excruciating detail how slaves were subjected to cruel punishments, how married couples were forcibly separated, etc.

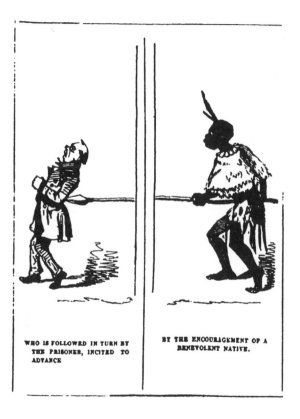

WHO IS FOLLOWED IN TURN BY THE PRISONER, INCITED TO ADVANCE

BY THE ENCOURAGEMENT OF A BENEVOLENT NATIVE.

t is hard to tell exactly when individualized Black characters began to appear in comics. No thorough research has been done to answer the question – as least so far as I am aware – and my own investigation has largely been limited to later book collections of vintage comics material. Even so, it is clear that Black characters – when they first showed up – overwhelmingly did so in the guise of the native stereotype. Sometimes the characters were "tame" savages, kidnapped and educated Africans housed in European royal courts. More often, though, native characters simply reflected crude European visualizations of Africans at home. The picture at left is from the third part of *The Surprising Adventures of Mr. Touchango Jones, an Emigrant*, by Albert Smith and H. G. Hine. Consisting of five installments, the series – from 1848 – was published at the rate of one page per month in the English humor magazine *Man In The Moon*. Touchango Jones is captured by savages, but naturally (!) their king's wife falls in love with him. Jones "righteously" kills her husband and is then proclaimed the new king of Quashybungo.

10 SLOPER improves the native mind. He teaches the simple savage a pretty little game with three thimbles and a pea.

Ally Sloper is often considered the first recurring character in European comics. Sloper himself represented a classic British archetype: the friendly, decidedly proletarian con man, cheating and swindling his way through life. From their start in 1867, his misadventures satirized both the pomp of the service sector and the unintentional self-deception of the lower-to-middle classes (the series' target audience). Sloper was conceived by the dramatist, comic novelist, and former civil servant Charles Henry Ross and developed and drawn by Ross's wife Marie Duval. The episode pictured opposite, "**Sloper In Savage Africa**," was published in the humor magazine *Judy, or the London Serio-Comic Journal* in 1872. Mocking British imperialism, the story shows Sloper setting out to "civilize" the natives by – among other pursuits – teaching them the old shell game. Sloper also takes an African wife, despite being a married man back home in England. "Perhaps," he comments afterwards, "one must conform to the customs of the country. Only she might have been a little better looking."

To push it home wheelbarrow-wise.
This huntsman wears a nasal ring
(For smartness more than anything).

The German artist Wilhelm Busch is one of the seminal creators in the history of comics. Working for German humor magazines in the late 1800s, Busch created numerous picture stories that have been translated and published worldwide to this day. Busch's most popular characters, Max and Moritz, were the direct progenitors of the long-running American comic strip *The Katzenjammer Kids* (see page 69). The image comes from the one-shot serial "**Fipps der Affe**" (Fipps the Monkey, 1879). The monkey eludes capture by grabbing his captor's nose ring in his tail; the sequence ends with the man's nose being forcibly ripped off. While the "gag" may seem extremely violent, here it reflects both a once-common European folk metaphor for castration and the nose's basic timelessness as a source of humor. The "Fipps" image as reproduced here is taken from the American volume *The Genius of Wilhelm Busch*, edited by Walter Arndt. Translating the story, Arndt in 1982 replaced the German equivalent of "Negro" (and, later, "wicked man") with the – for the time – more acceptable "huntsman."

— Oui, mes négrillots chéris, bon frère blanc vous apporte la civilisation... en bouteilles !...

The second half of the 19th century saw both a new wave of European colonization in Africa and a series of disputes between competing imperial powers. These incidents for the first time brought comics' political engagement to the international level – a level on which comics' sister art form, the magazine cartoon, had already functioned for a while. The image to the left is from **"Civilisons l'Afrique!"** (Let's Civilize Africa!), a sequence drawn by the cartoonist Camileff for the French humor magazine *L'Image pour Rire* in 1893. The caption says "Yes, my darling *négrillons* [literally piccaninnies], good white brother brings you civilization... in bottles!" The statement probably mirrored the readers' thoughts on this new wave of imperialism. These humor magazines' lower- to middle-class target group may have regarded Africans in a condescending manner, but they were simultaneously ambivalent – to say the least – as to whether colonial war was justifiable. The comic continues with the natives being slaughtered, cut down by bayonets, and shot to pieces by cannons.

52

While European cartoonists made fun of African colonial subjects, American comics often caricatured African-Americans. An early cartoonist to follow this trend was Richard F. Outcault. In his variously titled *Yellow Kid* pages, starting in 1895, Outcault featured a tough Black boy – eventually named the New Bully – as the Yellow Kid's fighting rival. A razor-swinging buck stereotype, Bully briefly starred in the spin-off strip *The Huckleberry Volunteers*, but it was not successful. The picture is from ***Poor Li'l Mose***, a marginally more successful series created by Outcault in 1901. Mose, a raggedy Black farm lad, was popular enough to headline a 1902 book collection. But when Outcault traded Mose for the new feature *Buster Brown*, with an upper-class white boy in the starring role, the result was a much bigger hit. Overzealous American comics historians used to call Richard F. Outcault the inventor of comics, but more thorough research has shown that the comics form preceded him by some time. The question of how *much* time depends on how you define comics.

54

George Herriman was one of the truly exceptional cartoonists in America at the dawn of the 20th century. His absurdist masterpiece *Krazy Kat* is still generally considered the best comic strip of all time. Even though Krazy herself (himself?) is sometimes claimed to represent a Black person, I would like to focus on *Musical Mose*, a short-lived series that Herriman created in 1902. Mose was a poor Black musician trying to make a living by performing in disguise at ethnic gatherings. But Mose's true ethnicity was always revealed, after which he was chased away by enraged spectators. The episode that starts with the panel to the left ends with Mose returning to Sal who asks him, "Why didn't yo impussanate a cannibal?" Herriman was himself partly Black, but tried his best never to reveal it to the public; for instance, he rarely allowed himself to be photographed without his hat, because he considered his hair "kinky." That Herriman worked in a business where it was a problem to be Black does not make *Musical Mose* – or its theme of trying to fit in – any less interesting.

56

Frederick Burr Opper was an American immigrant from Austria who became one of the most successful early 20th century cartoonists. Opper's most popular strip was *Happy Hooligan*, starring an optimistic, happy-go-lucky tramp made instantly recognizable by his distinctive tin-can cap. Happy was such a hit that his supporting cast — among others, the two overpolite Frenchmen Alphonse and Gaston — were awarded spin-off strips of their own. The panel is taken from a 1903 Sunday continuity called "**Alphonse, Gaston and Their Friend Leon In Darkest Africa.**" The main characters are exposed to Black native stereotypes who either want to eat them or make them kings, the latter solely based on the fact that they are white. To get away from the devout savages, Leon (being crowned in the picture to the left) claims to be a powerful magician and promises to make the sun crack into eight thousand pieces. The savages willingly gather around to look at the setting sun — and are still standing and staring sunward in the last panel of the strip, at which point the main characters have long since escaped to safety.

58

Winsor McCay was in the early 20th century one of the most respected creators working in comics. Today McCay is mostly remembered for *Little Nemo in Slumberland*, a very well-drawn Sunday strip about a boy experiencing fantastic adventures in his dreams. The series began in 1905; a short way into its run, a co-star called the Jungle Imp joined Nemo's retinue. The Imp had dark skin, spoke gibberish, wore a grass skirt, and had huge lips – in short, many characteristics of the native stereotype. Nemo met the Imp while visiting Slumberland's "Candy Islands," a region quite obviously inspired by Africa. The panel shows a party held there in Nemo's honor. Notice that all the Black characters look identical. One could excuse such a portrayal by saying that in a humorous comic strip everything is caricatured, or that in a dream world everything is distorted. The truth of the matter, though, is probably that it was considered perfectly all right to present Africans this way at the time. When Nemo was updated for an animated feature in the 1980s, the Imp's brown skin was turned blue.

60

n 1905 the T. C. McClure newspaper syndicate began to distribute *Sambo and His Funny Noises*, a strip created by the American William Marriner. The strip generally set Black boy Sambo Johnson (or Johnsin) against two white boy adversaries, Mike and Jim Tanks. Sambo often comes out on top in the skirmishes, but due more often to dumb luck, or to a "natural" ability to absorb pain, than to any intentional breaking of stereotypes. Marriner was a veteran of the humor magazine *Judge*. In it he had created a series of cartoons depicting Blacks as lazy, violent, superstitious, razor-wielding characters with pretensions to religion and Shakespeare; in short, an uninspired rehash of the era's stereotypes. The panel to the left comes from a late-1914 strip published shortly after Marriner's death. The dialogue seems prophetic when one looks at how Black characters in comics would later develop. Indeed, on the rare occasions when Marriner's assistant Pat Sullivan wrote and drew a Sambo strip on his own, Sambo at times became tellingly smarter and more independent.

When it comes to comics and almost everything else, the South American continent is often seen as standing in its big northern brother's shadow. There are, however, thriving comics cultures in several of the southerly continent's countries. That this is not a new phenomenon is proven, for example, by the surprisingly modern *Las Aventuras del Negro Raul* (The Adventures of the Black Man Raul), which was first published in 1916. *Raul* was printed in *El Hogar*, a daily journal in Buenos Aires, and created by the Argentinian Arturo Lanteri. The protagonist, Raul, lived in a threatening, pronouncedly racist world, and could only escape in his dreams to an existence in which he was rich and respected. In accordance with other cartoonists of the time, Lanteri placed the stories' text below the panels and always included a moral; though in contrast with Lanteri's contemporaries, the moral was generally bitter and cynical rather than uplifting. Daydreaming Raul's nonintegrated existence was ahead of its time – as is obvious if one compares it to the other comics I have chosen from this period.

64

One of the most popular fictional characters of the 1920s was *Felix the Cat*, created by Otto Messmer for the Pat Sullivan studio. Felix's screen debut came in 1919 and in August 1923 a comic strip was added. The panel is from 1925 and contains a mammy stereotype, but she pales beside Felix himself as the strip's principal Black image. Black, that is to say, by proxy. As it became too problematic to present traditional 19th-century Black stereotypes in the 20th century, it can be argued that aspects of the stereotypes were transferred to funny animals such as Krazy Kat, Felix, and later Mickey Mouse. It might be too bold to say that Felix is just a deracialized, feline Sambo Johnson, but Felix's narrow escapes often do tend to rely on Sambo's brand of dumb luck. The connection between Felix and Sambo runs deeper, too. Felix studio boss Pat Sullivan assisted William Marriner on the *Sambo* strip; Sullivan's first success in animation was a *Sambo* adaptation (renamed "Sammy Johnsin"). Only three years separate Sambo from Felix on the screen, and in the first Felix comics, the two would occasionally team up.

Niggeren: Den lille tykke er go'. Ha! Ha! — Og lidt
Kød er der vel ogsaa paa den lange. Ha! Ha!

The film medium in the silent era was not as dominated by English-speaking production houses as it would later become. In this context, a Danish film series could – and did – achieve international success. The comic duo of *Fyrtaarnet og Bivognen* (Lighthouse and Sidecar) debuted in 1920. The series, known for its influence on the later Laurel and Hardy, numbered about fifty films, most featuring Carl Schenstrøm as the thin, tall Ole and Harald Madsen as the short, chunky Axel. A spin-off comic strip appeared just two years after the films' debut; it would go on to outlast them, surviving until 1968. The comic went through several different hands over its first few years, but in 1924, the advertising illustrator Carl Røgind began a tenure that lasted until his death nine years later. Røgind was one of the first Danes to enter the comics medium. The panel to the left, from a 1933 *Fyrtaarnet* sequence, shows Ole and Axel having fallen into the clutches of typical native stereotypes. The caption says: "The nigger [sic]: The small fat one is alright! Ha! Ha! – And there is some meat on the tall one as well. Ha! Ha!"

68

German-American cartoonist Rudolph Dirks created *The Katzenjammer Kids* in 1897, and it is today the oldest comic strip still being produced. In fact, for quite a while it was two comic strips. A 1914 legal quarrel over the rights to the series saw Dirks and his publisher, Hearst, each granted permission to continue the series independently. *The Katzenjammer Kids* and *Captain and the Kids* strips ran simultaneously for decades afterward. Both series dealt with a German family living on the tropical Squee-Jee Island. The island's natives have a stereotypical outward appearance, but behave as fairly smart folk and speak grammatical English, in sharp contrast to the broken dialect of the dysfunctional Katzenjammers. Island king Bombo is a sophisticated, educated fellow who plays British sports such as cricket and golf. All of this was to some degree intended as an inverse parody of the standard native stereotype; but no matter the intent, the result was an early example of Black characters treated as equals. The panel is from 1928, and is the work of Harold Knerr – the artist hired by Hearst to replace Dirks.

70

Stereotypical Black characters were often given a type of "funny" dialect in American radio dramas, films, books, and – naturally – comics. In the panel to the left, a taxi driver expresses himself in typical exaggerated idiom; it might not surprise one to learn that white characters in the same strip spoke grammatically correct dialogue without the phonetic embellishment. Admittedly, such stark contrasts were not always the case. In the early days of American comics, it was fairly common for some white characters, too, to speak in exaggerated dialect – in their case representing the broken English of various immigrant populations. The panel is a 1928 example from the strip *Moon Mullins* by Frank Willard. A renowned figure of fun in his day – to the point of being immortalized in popular song – Mullins's titular ne'er-do-well lived in spinster Emily Schmaltz's run-down boarding house. This boarding house was populated with a diverse bunch of losers mostly derived from the bottom of society's pecking order. Black people, however, were noticeable by their absence from the roll call.

mmigrants were a prime target audience for early American comics, in part because they were expected to appreciate the simple language and direct humor the form supplied. Thus it was that Irishmen, Germans, Italians, and others, typically supplied with colorful dialect, could be major co-stars in strips whose central figures were white. Blacks, however, were almost always supporting players at best. As servants, maids, janitors, bellhops, and the like, the characters took menial roles similar to those they were locked into on the screen. The panel to the left is a 1929 example from Charles William Kahles's *Hairbreadth Harry*. Like several of its contemporaries, *Harry* built on the then-current popularity of movie serials, and their frequently contrived cliffhanger endings. The "Black maid" seen here happens to be a costumed white man, illustrating minstrelsy, a then-common entertainment trend rooted in 19th-century theater. White men blackened their faces with cork to sing and dance on the stage, intentionally or unintentionally ridiculing Black and poor white American lifestyles.

2-11

74

At its inception the *Mickey Mouse* daily strip was an exciting adventure serial set in exotic environments, with dangerous villains and fast-paced action. In the 1950s it became a family-oriented gag-a-day strip, centered on lightly humorous city life. Considering that the early Mickey, like Felix the Cat, had arguably embodied some characteristics of Black stereotypes, one might view the strip's transformation as Disney's "whitening" of the Mickey figure as he became an American icon. This panel comes from 1930, the comic's first year, when desert island travels lead Mickey to conflict with stereotypical cannibal natives. The cannibals at times have Mickey in a pickle, but he manages – as a representative of the Western world, his black skin notwithstanding – to fool them. The Walt Disney Company for a long time banned this sequence from being reprinted in any form, despite the fact that is is one of the few Mickey cointinuities actually written by Walt himself. Clearly, neither he nor artist Win Smith viewed the content as offensive at the time.

76

Georges Remi – or as he is better known, Hergé, the Belgian grandmaster of European cartoonists – was asked by his editor to create a serialized comics story about the Belgian colony of Congo. The result was *Tintin au Congo* (Tintin in the Congo), the second Tintin serial, published in 1930 and 1931. As Hergé later commented, it is a story full of racial stereotypes: "I didn't know anything more about the country than what people were saying at the time. The Negroes are like big children; how lucky it is for them that we are there!" Congolese Africans are presented as primitive, gullible natives, prone to worshipping the white man. Even in later Tintin continuities, wherein Hergé tried to adopt a more humane point of view, racial stereotypes continue to turn up. In 1958's *Coke en stock* (The Red Sea Sharks), Tintin battles to expose modern-day slave traders and free their victims – Black Muslims who only think they are going to Mecca. Unfortunately the Blacks are still depicted as stereotypical, somewhat naive and foolish, with big lips and dialogue such as: "Us good Muslim. Us want to go to Mecca."

78

Comic strips that have existed for a very long time have often found it necessary to mutate to adapt to our ever-changing world. One such strip is *Gasoline Alley*, initiated in 1918 by Frank O. King and continued to date by a succession of creators. This humorous story of life in an American small town is unique in that its characters age in step with the strip's readers. This aspect, combined with King's (and his successors') constant efforts to capture the spirit of the times, makes *Gasoline Alley* ideal for a study of America's changing 20th-century values. The panel is from 1931 and depicts the maid Rachel. She is the epitome of the mammy stereotype, with her appearance and status evolving directly from the times of slavery. Much of the humor in the strip at this time arose from the conflict between Rachel . who had worked for the main character Walt Wallet in his bachelor days, and Walt's new wife Phyllis, who had new ideas about managing the household. Phyllis was always drawn in a realistic manner, pretty as a picture – a drawing style that starkly contrasted with Rachel and her caricatured looks.

"Or if I were a pirate, I know I'd be bold;
I'd bury a chest filled with silver and gold."

The late 1920s and early 1930s saw early efforts among Black Americans to protest against stereotyping in radio, movies, and cartoons. Into this climate came Hugh Harman and Rudy Ising's *Bosko* – the first Warner Brothers cartoon and comic star. Bosko began in 1929 as a bashful, silly coon stereotype, speaking in heavy dialect. But a change was made two films into the series (at Ising's initiative, according to his recollection, decades later): Bosko's dialect all but vanished and surprisingly progressive behavior took the place of clichés. Bosko took jobs such as cinema owner and restaurant boss, and he defended his girlfriend, Honey, from white villains. The panel to the left – drawn by Win Smith for a 1934 Sunday page – suggests the manner in which the character was developing. But just one year later progress reversed itself. Bosko moved to MGM and Harman gained sole director's duty, transforming his hero into a realistically drawn piccaninny stereotype. It was left for later hands to undo the damage, typically by reshowing only pre-1935 cartoons on TV and recasting Bosko as an animal figure for modern use.

I n 1934 the Americans Lee Falk and Phil Davis created the classic adventure strip *Mandrake the Magician*. It is a comic in which everyone has his place: well-dressed prestidigitator, adventurer, and gentleman Mandrake is backed up by the strong, silent, none-too-intelligent Black servant Lothar, a stereotypical native in costume and tom in behavior. As originally conceived, Lothar provided the laughs in *Mandrake*, confronting Western cultural traditions, and invariably winding up at a loss. The panel to the left is from the strip's second Sunday page, published in 1935, at which point Lothar was physically more exaggerated than he would later become. As the years passed – and American racial consciousness evolved – Lothar evolved as well. Revealed as the son of a king in his native land, Mandrake's servant became more and more an equal to the magician. Lothar lost his exaggerated lips, broken English, and lionskin garment – the latter swapped for jeans and a T-shirt. In theory, Lothar ultimately did become his master's equal. In practice, and in spite of good intentions, old habits die hard.

The notion of Blacks as superstitious was often used as a humorous element in early American movies, novels, and comics. One comic to follow the trend was the daily strip *Minute Movies*, created by the cartoonist Ed Wheelan and published in Hearst newspapers between 1921 and 1936. *Minute*'s conceit was to treat each strip as one chapter in an imaginary movie serial – a serial complete with cast, crew, director, and so forth. Wheelan utilized this format to make fun of the film industry, give "awards" to fictional actors, have his characters write movie reviews, and spoof almost every contemporary film genre. "Planet Plans," the serial pictured to the left, dates from 1935 and tells the story of a group of people attempting to fly to Pluto. Among the motley crew are inventor Horace Hooey, his beautiful wife and secretary Carrie Carbon, billionaire playboy Red Rash, and Red's faithful Black servant Plato Bean. The "role" of Bean – "acted" by *Minute Movies* player "Charcoal" Burn – contributes the stereotypical humorous traits of superstition, cowardice, and colorful language.

Two years after creating *Mandrake* – that is to say, in 1936 – Lee Falk also created the comic strip ***The Phantom***. The panel opposite is drawn by Ray Moore and taken from the very first year of the series. *The Phantom*'s basic premise – that a white man in the jungle protects simple savages by spreading law and order – was probably a fully acceptable concept in 1930s America. The strip has changed considerably over the years – not least during the 1960s and 1970s, when its theme drifted out of touch with prevailing social mores. Today most new *Phantom* comics are written and produced in Sweden – a country known for its struggles on behalf of equality – so it is perhaps not surprising that the Phantom's jungle now numbers an elected Black leader and democratic rule. In essence, the comic's more recent creators have tried to adjust an inherently imperialist concept to fit more modern methods of thought. Even so, the Phantom is still waited upon by the pygmy Bandar people; and their leader, Guran, while highly educated, is implicitly never quite the equal of his big white friend.

„Hoe kom je nu weer aan dat witte oog, Simmie? Zeker weer gevochten, hè?"

S ometimes comics characters develop in an unforeseen direction, seemingly with a will of their own. This is the case with *Sjors en Sjimmie* (George and Jimmy), one of Holland's most successful strips. White boy Perry Winkle debuted in *Winnie Winkle, the Breadwinner*, a comic strip created by the American cartoonist Martin Branner in 1920, and became the strip's title character in the Netherlands, where local translators called him Sjors (i.e. George). When a Dutch comics magazine needed original material, local production of *Sjors* stories began. Then Branner in the 1940s chose to remove Perry from *Winnie Winkle* – leaving the Dutch free to develop Perry their own way. It was now that a friend of Perry's, the piccaninny stereotype Sjimmie, shook his clichéd origins to become the comic's second star. Sjimmie also became Perry's full equal – a status underlined by his sharing of the strip's title from the 1960s. The panel to the left, drawn by Frans Piët in 1937, shows Sjimmie long before his transformation. "Where did you get that white eye, Sjimmie?" asks mammy. "Have you been fighting again?"

10. And she made signs to Smudgie that she wanted him to dance with her. "Suits me, lady, " chortled the chocolate drop cheerily. " I'se a dab at dis dance ! Music, please, professor ! " he chucled to the conductor. Then they danced.

One finds plenty of stereotyped, grass-skirted natives when looking through old English comics. Also common is the piccaninny, most typically presented as the "colorful" Black child in an otherwise white kid gang. A minority member could eke equality out of such a position – but only up to a point. *The Jolly Antics of Smiler and Smudge, The Comical Couple of Carraway College*, from *Butterfly* (reportedly the first British humor magazine to present Black citizens as equals), exemplifies this. It featured two friends – one white boy and one Black (no prizes for guessing who was who). The pair attended an English college together, indicating a progressive streak. Creator Bertie Brown also let Smudge get the better of Smiler, often walking off with the pretty girl. But the characters' true equality was questionable. The panel to the left is from 1939. Smudge meets a trained female monkey who takes a shine to him(!). Smudge and the monkey are drawn very similarly, and he is referred to as "half-size of Blacking," "Black blob," "coon," "inkspot," "darkie," and "chocolate drop" in the course of the story.

Will Eisner is one of the great creators in the comics medium, with the weekly newspaper supplement *The Spirit* arguably his crowning achievement. First presented to the public in 1940, The Spirit was a masked crime fighter with the Black youth Ebony White as his sidekick. As indicated by his name, the latter began his career as a traditional Black supporting character and, with his balloon lips and Southern drawl, represented a very conscious use of classical stereotype. Eisner himself said of Ebony's creation: "I realize that Ebony was a stereotype because I drew him in caricature – but how else could I have treated a black boy in that era, at that time?" Ebony gradually developed into more than just a humble sidekick, however. A change is especially visible when Eisner returned to the series after his service in World War II; Ebony received a more pronounced and equal role, and new Black characters were introduced to the strip. Among them was detective Lt. Grey, who was drawn in a more realistic way and spoke grammatically correct English, without any trace of Southern dialect.

94

During the 1940s more and more American comics were created directly for comic books – periodicals that, until not long before, had been dominated by reprints of newspaper strips. *Pat, Patsy and Pete* was created by Win Smith, then continued by others directly for Dell's *Looney Tunes and Merrie Melodies Comics*. Pat and Patsy were two children who traveled the world with their talking penguin Pete. This panel comes from 1942, when the trio wound up on a nearly deserted atoll with two human inhabitants, castaway sailor Jack Tar and Hokery Pokery, "the only cannibal on this island." The latter was a combination of the native and the coon stereotypes – full of mischief and prone to linguistic lapses. Hokery's pidgin English was characterized by the random addition of the suffix "-ry"; in one story, this was taken to mean that his given name might be Hokey Pokey, but that he could not pronounce it. Hokery also spoke in rhyme, further emphasizing his childish nature. When Walt Kelly (*Pogo*), a more socially conscious cartoonist, took over the series in 1943 he immediately removed Hokery.

Another interesting feature from American children's comics was *Li'l Eight Ball*, based on a short-lived Walter Lantz animated cartoon character from the late 1930s. The panel to the left is from a 1942 issue of *New Funnies*, and was probably drawn by Dan Gormley (the artists were not allowed to sign their work). The title character, on-screen a nightgown-clad wise guy with an improbably adult Mel Blanc voice, became in the comics a classical piccaninny stereotype. The feature began as a simple slapstick comedy set in the rural South with Eight Ball, his "Mammy," and a family of hillbilly woodchucks as the only recurring figures. After a while, however, a larger Black human society grew around Eight Ball. Along with girlfriend Honeysuckle Jones and rival Shadrack Paducah, one could find some unusual compound stereotypes – Black Irish policemen, for example. It was a caricatured world doomed to become too awkward for its times. In 1947 Eight Ball's Southern dialect was replaced with highly grammatical English; a short time later the strip itself disappeared.

Walt Kelly's daily strip *Pogo* began in 1948. With its mix of anthropomorphic animals, wild humor, and political satire, the series is counted today as one of the true classics of comics. Pogo Possum, Albert the Alligator, and others live in a version of Georgia's Okefenokee Swamp that is "peopled" exclusively with critters. Yet it was not always so. Long before 1948, Kelly created children's comics in which early versions of Pogo and his pals coexisted with humans, a young Black boy named Bumbazine chief among them. The panel is from **"Bumbazine and Albert in an Adventure with the Half-Jug Family,"** published in 1943 in *Our Gang Comics*. Some have objected to Kelly's choice of a Black boy to talk with the animals, but one must consider that Kelly portrayed the beasts in question as ridiculous caricatures. Bumbazine was, by comparison, the most normal of the crew; his Southern accent at its thickest is consciously less extreme than the animals'. In truth, the politically conscious and openly liberal Kelly was a pioneer in allowing Black characters as equals in mass-market American comics.

The comic most people remember when thinking of the native stereotype is probably *Tarzan*. The American Edgar Rice Burroughs based his novels on the marvelous idea of a child being raised by the noble animals in the African jungle; there is, however – as with *The Phantom* – an undeniable imperialism behind the notion that the white Tarzan should quite naturally rule over Black human "savages." Burroughs's books spawned, among other spin-offs, an adventure strip beginning in 1929 that is today considered a classic. The panel is from 1945, drawn by Burne Hogarth – known for his anatomically realistic figure drawing. Hogarth's correctness extended to the Africans, who on a purely visual level looked more real than many of their large-lipped contemporaries in comics. They were, however, extremely stereotypical in their behavior and personalities – so much so that the strip was criticized in its day by African delegates to the United Nations. *Tarzan* presented, they felt, the image of Africa as a one-nation continent, consisting entirely of jungles inhabited by uneducated savages.

Most Black characters in comics were still given very stereotypical features, and roles, in the 1940s. There were exceptions, though; one of them being an untitled story published in *World's Finest* #17, from 1945 – written by Jack Schiff and drawn by John Daly. Sgt. Ralph Jackson leads a battallion of Black American soldiers against the Nazis. After heroically shooting down an attacking Messerschmitt while wounded, he is awarded both the Silver Star and the Purple Heart. When arriving in the U.S.A., though, he is turned away from several restaurants. Finally he is allowed in, when a white friend, Johny "Everyman," invites him. Considering the way Black people were treated in most other popular media of the time, this is a bold statement about the hypocrisy of fighting bigotry overseas while it is being practiced at home. That it was meant that way is confirmed by the text: "Dedicated to the millions of American Negroes who are doing their share in the armed forces and on the home front to win the war and usher in a new era of peace and understanding among men."

American objections to stereotyping in the media grew noticeably in the postwar years. In response, some clichéd figures were modified. Mammy Two-Shoes had been a part of William Hanna and Joe Barbera's *Tom and Jerry* from its start as an MGM cartoon in 1940, and a comic book in 1942. Mammy debuted as a generic mammy stereotype complete with comic dialect and servile status, her only distinction being that her face was never seen. Though she disciplined "Thomas" with an iron broom, it was clear – particularly in the comics – that she did so on her employers' behalf. But time changes everything. In the late 1940s the white folks vanished, with Mammy turning mistress in their place. She suddenly slept in a big bedroom, dressed up for evenings at the club, and managed the expense account. Her personality changed from that of patsy to long-suffering cynic. 1960s *Tom and Jerry* creators went further, dropping Mammy or recoloring her white; but today the original Black character is seen again. The panel is from a 1949 issue of *Our Gang*, drawn by Harvey Eisenberg.

Hon hängde, klättrade och hoppa
betydligt bättre än en loppa.

Herr Tupp (Mr. Rooster) and his family were the main characters in a series of 1940s and 1950s Swedish advertising giveaways. The giveaways' stories, told in simple picture sequences with rhymed texts beneath, were created for *Tuppens Väv* (Rooster's Fabric) by the artist Erik Persson and the writer Gunnar Wersén. In *Herr Tupp*'s second issue, the chicken family meets Black girl Hilda during a trip to an exotic island – and simply decides to take her with them. In the third issue, **"Kuckeliku och Hilda i skolan"** (Cock-A-Doodle-Doo and Hilda at School), from 1949, Hilda is the main character. She goes to school and the humor derives from her not being like everybody else; the teacher, for example, offers a self-assured judgment after a quick glance: "She seems a bit behind, that Hilda." One interesting aspect of *Herr Tupp* is that Hilda is the only human character in an otherwise animal world. Evidently, a Black person was by her very nature unusual enough to fit right in among birds in clothes. The text under the panel to the left says that Hilda "hung, climbed, and jumped considerably better than a flea."

108

Disney Duck Man Carl Barks was one of the truly great storytellers in comics; many of his tales are considered indisputable classics. Although Barks created most of his canon in the 1940s and 1950s, thanks to their timeless quality most of his stories read as well today as they ever did. Yet a small number of Barks creations have been outpaced by the ages. The panel to the left is taken from "**Voodoo Hoodoo**," published in Dell's *Four Color* #238 from 1949. In it, Donald and his nephews travel to Africa, where they meet native stereotypes complete with grass skirts, extremely exaggerated lips, and Southern dialect. "Voodoo Hoodoo" was kept out of circulation for close to 40 years, and when it reappeared American editors adjusted it to suit current readers. Dialect was altered, sharpened teeth flattened, and nose rings plucked from the Africans; Bop Bop, Donald's jazz musician friend back home in Duckburg, was changed from Black to white. Big lips were also replaced – to grotesque effect for a few characters, whose newly drawn mouths have no lips whatsoever. (The 2011 Fantagraphics Barks Library edition restored the initial version.)

The image to the left comes from *Kimba the White Lion*, by Osamu Tezuka. Known as the king of Japanese comics, Tezuka can – with his immense production of both comics and animation that have saturated Japanese culture – in American terms be compared only to Walt Disney. *Kimba* was created in 1950, a period when Black characters were not that common in Japanese comics; this is not so strange when one realizes that Japan at the time had almost no immigrants whatsoever. When Black characters did appear, they usually took stereotypical forms that the Japanese had encountered in American comics during the first half of the century. Funny animals were often Black-skinned characters, but likely derived without an understanding of the images' background. Black humans were grass-skirted cannibal natives with bones in their noses, servile servants, or maybe – at best – jazz musicians. As for Tezuka's *Kimba*, it has turned the tables to influence American culture; not least by way of Disney's *The Lion King* (1994), in some ways derivative of *Kimba* (in spite of the Disney executives' fervent denials).

From 1936 to the mid-1960s the Swedish comic strip *Biffen och Bananen* (Beefsteak and Banana) was written and drawn by Jan-Erik "Rit-Ola" Garland and published in the magazine *Folket i Bild*. The panel comes from about 1950 – when it was evidently acceptable to depict native Africans with pitch-black faces and big lips, ready to carry out menial tasks for white folks (the word balloon reads: "Hello, all Negroes! Run and hide behind the embankment!"). Rit-Ola was known in public life for his outspoken social consciousness and progressive political stance, so one would imagine his use of stereotype to reflect the spirit of the times, rather than any personal prejudice. Nevertheless, his racial humor could be strikingly insensitive. In another strip of the period Rit-Ola illustrates an African banquet, where "unusual" foods (snails, grasshoppers, and the like) and clothing provide the humor. Admittedly, there is some effort to present the banquet's guests as nuanced, normal people. It is hard to seem normal, however, when one speaks broken dialect and has a crudely caricatured face.

There are numerous examples of horribly stereotypical Black characters in European comics from the first half of the 20th century, but also examples of the opposite. *Blondin et Cirage* (Blondie and Shoeshine) by the great Belgian cartoonist Jijé (Joseph Gillain) is a famous example of an early French-Belgian comic with a Black character that is not a stereotype. The comic was actually created, or so the myth goes, by Jijé in 1939 because he was appalled by the paternalistic way in which Black people were treated in Hergé's *Tintin in the Congo*. Both Blondin and Cirage are visual caricatures, but even though Blondin is often shown as the more intelligent of the two, it is evident that Cirage is the main protagonist and the one who solves the problems they are faced with. In ***Silence on Tourne!*** (Quiet on the Set!) from 1952, the boys realize that there is money to be made from radio show quizzes, but it is Cirage who studies assiduously (he is shown poring over the great French encyclopedia of the time) and wins all the money. The lazy Blondin "only" reads the magazine *Spirou*, in which their comic was published…

The comics I have analyzed in this book so far, mostly the work of white creators, cannot and do not represent the entirety of the Black experience in classic comics. Running concurrently with white-created strips were Black-created strips, produced for Black-owned syndicates and papers. As one might expect, the Black characters in these strips were not locked into stereotypical savage or sidekick roles. Instead, they were the stars of highly varied detective, science fiction, Wild West, and romance sagas. While much has yet to be learned about early Black-created comics, Jackie Ormes was almost certainly the first syndicated Black female cartoonist. Ormes's strip, *Torchy Brown*, was distributed from 1937 on by the Afro-American Continental Features Syndicate. Torchy was an intelligent, self-reliant Black career woman, whose stories showed her fighting racism, sex discrimination, and environmental hazards. As a positive role model for Black women, Torchy clashed with the servile mammies of the era's white-created comics. The panel comes from the series' second run, in the 1950s.

AND INSIDE THE SHIP, THE MAN REMOVED HIS SPACE HELMET AND SHOOK HIS HEAD, AND THE INSTRUMENT LIGHTS MADE THE BEADS OF PERSPIRATION ON HIS DARK SKIN TWINKLE LIKE DISTANT STARS...

THE END

7

Self-proclaimed guardians of 1950s American public morality mounted numerous campaigns against comic books. The publisher Entertaining Comics (EC) was the campaigns' most famous casualty. Working within "lowbrow" genres such as horror, war, and science fiction, EC's authors told stories that are today regarded as classics. Nevertheless, the era's critics deemed them too violent. To ward off attack, EC signed up with the Comics Code Authority, the new comics censorship board. However, the Code's reactionary ideas made for a short-lived relationship. The panel is from "**Judgement Day**" – written by Bill Gaines and Al Feldstein, and drawn by Joe Orlando. An astronaut visits a planet of orange and blue robots; he witnesses the robots' mutual prejudice and concludes that the planet is not ready for admission into the Galactic Empire. Returning home, the astronaut takes off his helmet to reveal himself as a Black man. In 1956 the Code's censors objected to this final image; a stubborn Gaines published the story, which was actually a reprint from *Weird Fantasy*, in *Incredible Science Fiction* with no changes.

The Belgian cartoonist André Franquin is one of the defining figures in European comics culture, and the series *Spirou et Fantasio* – on which he worked from 1946 to 1968 – is a classic in the comedy-adventure genre. Most of the albums in Franquin's large production have been published throughout Europe, but the story "**Tembo Tabou**," originally serialized in 1959, has been avoided by several countries (and was only released in album form in France and Belgium much later) – possibly because the publishers were concerned about the racist imagery. The story, written by Greg (Michel Regnier) and co-drawn by Jean Roba, about the two white heroes who visit the jungle and meet pygmies, is full of racial caricatures – but rather charming ones, at that. It is easy to draw parallels between the tiny, identical pygmies and the little, blue Smurfs (who debuted at about the same time in the same magazine). Other albums by Franquin contain equally caricatured representations of Africans – for example *La Corne du Rhinocéros* (The Rhinoceros's Horn) – but escaped censorship or suppression.

Another comic printed in the Black press was *Tommy Traveller in the World of Negro History*, by the Black cartoonist Tom Feelings. It was published in the Harlem-based *New York Age* between 1958 and 1959, and the main character was a small Black boy engaged in his favorite activity – reading and dreaming himself into the settings of Black American history. This comic entered the scene in a time when America was filled with civil rights protests, boycotts and student sit-ins – something that could explain the "daring" way in which Feelings portrayed the Black characters, with for instance "natural" hairstyles. The latter might seem trivial, but *Tommy Traveller* was very much before its time, since comics in main American magazines of this era still featured Black characters as servants, jazz musicians, etc. – if they were shown at all. Episodes from *Tommy Traveller* were later reworked and used in the *Golden Legacy* series (see page 135). It is telling that when the strip finally was collected in a book of its own, as late as 1991, the word "Negro" in the title was replaced with "Black."

Rune Andréasson has often been called the Walt Disney of Sweden. The comparison stems from the fact that he created many children's comics and animated films with anthropomorphic characters. The panel is excerpted from the comic *Teddy*, published in 1960. This story took place in a "Negro village" in the "Unknown Jungle," and the heroes have been captured by some extremely stereotypical natives. Andréasson was otherwise known as a socially conscious person, who in his most famous creation, *Bamse*, during the 1970s, taught children about solidarity, equality, freedom from prejudices, etc. Maybe he was more naïve at the time, but the truth of the matter is probably that in 1960, it was still acceptable in Sweden to represent Africans in this way. When comparing this scene with another comic by Andréasson, *Habibu*, published thirteen years later, it is obvious that either Andréasson's or the society's values – or both – had changed. *Habibu* features a Black main character and presents a realistic view of the people of Africa, with racism and starving natives contrasted with rich tourists, etc.

Anthropomorphic comics, that is to say comics in which the characters are animals who act like people, are often a useful genre for dealing with subjects that can be hard to handle in a more realistic form. Comics where all characters are animals, and therefore can't be seen as belonging to a certain national group, are for example well suited for stories in which you either totally disregard the question of racism (as in the Disney comics), or raise it to a more allegorical plane. One comic which adopted the latter approach is the Dutch *Tom Poes*, which was started as a daily strip by Marten Toonder in 1938. The stories were often satirical and in the episode "**The Evil Eye**," from the beginning of the 1960s, Toonder tackled the subject of racism. The story dealt with the relationship between white and black sheep, where the blacks were seen as different and in possession of "the evil eye" (which caused accidents to happen). The myth said that it was the "black tongue" that caused all problems. A magical brew could cure this, but not until all *white* sheep had drunk it did the misunderstandings get cleared up...

128

Black soldiers have fought, and died, in many American wars, believing that their valor would finally make the white population see them as first class citizens. Some say that this is exactly what has happened, even though it took a long time; others say that it was all for nothing. Still, in comics, some of the earliest examples of stories featuring Black characters as equals were about war. One of these early stories was "**What's the Color of Your Blood?**,"published in *Our Army At War* #160, from 1965; written by Bob Kanigher and drawn by Joe Kubert, and featuring the Black soldier Jackie Johnson (presumably a reference to the first Black heavyweight champion Jack Johnson). In this story he fights a German prizefighter, who taunts him by saying that his blood is black. Jackie wins the fight and the Germans opens fire in dismay that their "Aryan" should lose to a Black man. The German fighter is the one who gets shot, though, and when he in the end is rescued by a blood transfusion by the only man present with his bloodtype, Jackie, he exclaims: "I was wrong. *Wrong!* The color of your blood... is... *red!*"

130

It has been said that one effect of the Americans realizing that Black soldiers had fought as valiantly as their white counterparts in WWII was that it became less acceptable to use Black stereotypes in popular culture. Whether this was true or not, at this time there *was* a growing movement for a more integrated society. As cartoonists seemingly did not know how to treat Black characters, they disappeared almost totally. The Black cartoonist Morrie Turner had an idea in the 1960s to make an integrated strip about children. He showed it to Charles M. Schulz – the creator of *Peanuts* – who gave it his full support; with this backing he managed to get it syndicated in 1965. The comic was called **Wee Pals** and featured children with various ethnic, religious, and cultural backgrounds, who mostly hang out like "ordinary comic kids." Initially it only ran in five newspapers, but the renewed interest in the situation of Blacks following the assassination of Martin Luther King, Jr. in 1968 gave the strip a boost. Within three months it was appearing in over 100 newspapers. Turner still writes and draws *Wee Pals* today.

Popular culture is adept at capturing the spirit of the time, and comics often provide good examples of this. In 1967, the Americans Gardner Fox, Mike Sekowsky, and Sid Greene created a *very* politically correct story in *Justice League of America* #57, "**Man, Thy Name Is – Brother!**" This contrived yarn has members of the League setting out to meet with people to gather information for a college paper on Brotherhood Week. The Flash meets the young Black man Joel Harper, who, when praised for saving the life of a clothing manufacturer, requests a job as a reward. A gang of thieves steals clothes from the manufacturer, and Harper's attempt to thwart them results in his firing. After being blinded, and having to rely on Harper's directions to catch the thieves, the Flash gives him the following advice: "I'm confident that some day you'll be a top-grade policeman – if you have the confidence and ambition to make a go of it." This is, to put it mildly, strange (and condescending) advice to give to a man who just stated his desire to work in the manufacturing business.

134

lassics Illustrated was a successful series of comic books, published between 1941 and 1969, which contained versions of famous books, plays, and events in history, in the form of comics. In the middle of the 1960s several Black American organizations collaborated on publishing *Golden Legacy*, a comic book whose aim was stated in the first page: "The subject of our magazine, Golden Legacy, is Black history and is written so young people can understand and develop interest for further study of Black history." In these magazines (16 were published between 1966 and 1972) were told the stories of famous Black inventors, explorers, authors, freedom fighters, et al. The picture is taken from the second issue: "**Harriet Tubman – the Moses of Her People**," by Joan Bachus and Tom Feelings (who earlier wrote and drew *Tommy Traveller in the World of Negro History*). These comics had the same basic idea of using comics in an educational way as *Classics Illustrated*; interestingly enough, the very last issue of the original series of *Classics Illustrated*, from 1969, was titled "Negro Americans: The Early Years"…

Since Superman's 1938 debut, the dominant genre in American comics has been superheroes. Despite this fact, and despite the large proportion of Black people in the U.S.A., there were for a long time no Black superheroes. The history of Stan Lee and Jack Kirby's character *The Black Panther* mirrors the changing times; introduced in 1966 in the comic *Fantastic Four*, he was for a while only one of the members of the superhero group The Avengers. The panel is from his second appearance in *Fantastic Four*, drawn by Kirby and inked by Joe Sinnott. The character eventually became an icon for the struggle against racism, sharing as he did a name with the '60s activist party the Black Panthers. (This was almost certainly a coincidence, since the group was formed later in the same year that the character made his first appearance.) Marvel responded to concern about the name issue by renaming the character "The Black Leopard" in the early 1970s, but this was short-lived: In 1973 he gained his own series in the magazine *Jungle Action* under his own name, and in 1977 he got his very own comic book.

The American Charles M. Schulz stirred up many emotions when he, in 1968, introduced the Black Franklin as a fully equal character in *Peanuts*, the world's most successful daily comic. However good his intentions, Schulz was subjected to heavy criticism from white *and* Black groups. It is probably symptomatic of Schulz's way of working that he did not make a big thing out of the introduction of this new character, but simply had him show up as a natural part of the comic. Schulz didn't give Franklin any distinctive characteristics based on his being Black, which is totally different from how many other comics artist have treated "their" Black character – who often have become a symbol of the whole Black community. Schulz actually took this one step further and often made the strips in which Franklin appeared without an obvious gag, something which indicates that he – when introducing this character – wasn't just looking for new jokes. The fact that Franklin doesn't have a pronounced personality actually makes him stand out among the other quite strong characters of the strip, though.

Robert Crumb is one of the true innovators of the comics in the second half of the 20th century. He is in a sense the Woody Allen of the field, with an intense need to reveal his innermost feelings in his work. Crumb was among the people who started underground comics in the United States, a movement that was part of the hippie era that swept the nation in the 1960s and was very much about breaking with all the written and unwritten laws. Crumb has during his long career broken many taboos, and it is therefore not surprising that he often used very stereotypical Black figures – which otherwise had disappeared from American comics. The panel is taken from the story "**Angelfood McSpade,**" from 1968. Angelfood was one of Crumb's recurring characters, and he has used several other Black characters – often with extremely stereotypical features. Some critics have seen this as evidence that he is a racist, but the truth of the matter is probably that he uses these charged images to provoke a reaction from the readers, forcing them to make up their own minds about their attitudes toward racism.

© Field Enterprises, Inc., 1968

A. Mc WILLIAMS
J. SAUNDERS
© PIB
COPENHAGEN

One of the first daily strips with a Black main character to be syndicated in major daily newspapers was *Dateline: Danger!* This comic was written by Allen Saunders and drawn by Alden McWilliams – and was a very typical product of its time. It was launched in 1968, when the integration of white and Black people in the United States was a hot-button issue. Hoping to regain some parts of the audience lost to other media, the creators chose to model their comic on the popular TV series "I Spy." Since this program featured a team consisting of one white and one Black character (the latter played by Bill Cosby), this also became the premise of the comic. Suitably enough the Black character was named Raven... The two reporters, who also worked as undercover agents for the American government, travelled around the world to report about, and unveil, various conspiracies. On the home front the story often dealt with how Danny Raven, with his sister and brother, stopped the Black extremist Robin Jackson's revolutionary plans. The strip was ended in 1974, when it had played out its role.

This panel is taken from the comic *Phoenix* by the Japanese cartoonist Osamu Tezuka. *Phoenix* is Tezuka's masterpiece – an ongoing story about immortality and the meaning of life. In this scene, from 1968, the main character is chased by the police through an overgrown area, and Tezuka included a stereotypical African native as a gag. At the time this was totally acceptable in Japan, even though it is obvious that these stereotypical images had been imported from American comics without the cartoonists thinking all that much about the social context in which they had been developed. In 1990 the "Association to Stop Racism against Blacks" started a campaign to put a stop to racism in manga. To the horror of many manga readers, this campaign focused on Tezuka, who was beloved in Japan for his compassion and humanism. Since Tezuka himself by this time was dead, his company decided not to alter his comics in the reprints, but added a disclaimer saying that while some images were drawn in a less-enlightened era, Tezuka himself had been adamantly opposed to racism in any form.

Yet another "early" strip containing Black characters that was syndicated to major newspapers was *Quincy*, by the cartoonist Ted Shearer. Shearer was asked by the syndicate King Features, probably since he himself was Black, to do a strip following the success of Turner's *Wee Pals*. *Quincy* was a humor strip, introduced in 1970, telling the story of a group of mostly Black, urban children. Even if Shearer didn't avoid subjects such as racism, segregation, and poverty he was never preachy; he showed a lot of the injustices that he and his children had lived through, but always let the readers make up their own minds. As Shearer himself put it, he had "been hurt many times... but I must always remind myself that I make a comic strip and not political cartoons." In the beginning Shearer was often criticized for not taking an open stand in questions concerning integration, but the strip has since been reappraised in comics history. What many comics historians miss, though, is the fact that even if *Quincy* may have broken new grounds, Shearer had been working as an artist in the Black press since 1937.

148

Daily comics published in newspapers are among the most conservative in the comics field. Very little variation is allowed and everything is expected to be as innocuous as possible – which often has resulted in the exclusion of Black characters. Two persons who reacted against this were the Americans Sid Jacobson and Ernie Colón. In 1970 they produced the book *The Black Comic Book* (with the words "Negro" and "Colored" crossed out in the title...). It contains parodies of well-known strips in which the main characters have been changed into Blacks, done in the brilliant way of simply applying a gray tint to their skin – and not altering anything else. Here you find old favorites such as "Bronzie" (*Blondie*), "Superblack" (*Superman*), "Raisins" (*Peanuts*), "Big Eboner" (*Li'l Abner*), and many more. In the introduction you can read that "This satire of America's best loved comic strips is presented strictly for laughs, but with the hope that one day – in a world of greater honesty, justice and understanding – the Black man will take his rightful place in literature of all kinds."

The first American daily strip to get its title from the name of a Black character and be syndicated to major newspapers was *Friday Foster*. It was also the first with a female Black main character. The strip debuted the 18th of January 1970, written by the (white) American Jim Lawrence and drawn by the Spaniard Jorge Longarón. Lawrence was an experienced scriptwriter who had written several comic strips, including *James Bond*, *Joe Palooka*, and *Captain Easy*, and who felt that there was a dearth of Black characters in daily strips. He therefore created Friday, a female fashion photographer, who travelled around the world and finally ended up being a model herself. Even if the main character was said to come from Harlem, and there were attempts to introduce more serious subjects, the story was mostly a soap opera and Friday only a beautiful Black woman who had succeeded in the world of white people; for the most part there were no other Black characters visible. The strip was cancelled in 1974, but a year later there was a filmed version, with the blaxploitation queen Pam Grier as Friday.

Superheroes as a genre can – at its better moments – be an interesting mirror of our own society. During the late 1960s and early 1970s there were a number of so-called "relevant" superhero comics. One of the the most talked about was *Green Lantern/Green Arrow*, written by Dennis O'Neil and drawn by Neal Adams. By combining two very different heroes and applying what Dick Giordano, the inker of the series, called the "we-care-about-important-issues-method," they managed to create something that was new and fresh for its time. The creators raised questions about drug abuse, street violence, poverty, and, of course, considering the racial tensions that ravaged the U.S.A. at this time, racism. The heroes got to fight a landlord who refused to renovate a building with poor, Black tenants, fail to save a Black boy from dying in a street fight, and appoint a Black character as the "temp" for the Green Lantern. The sequence to the left is from 1970 and was heard far outside of the usual comics community (which is why I have chosen to deviate from my own rule of only including one panel from each comic).

154

After Charles M. Schulz – the creator of *Peanuts* – had added a Black character to his strip's cast, several other cartoonists followed suit. Mort Walker introduced *his* Black character, Lt. Jack Flap, in the comic **Beetle Bailey** on the 5th of October 1970. He did this despite loud protests from the syndicate, who were afraid that it would cost them numerous subscribing newspapers. In contrast with Schulz, Walker made a clear statement with his character and gave him a personality based on the movements among Blacks of the time. This led to complaints from both Black groups – who thought they were being made fun of – and white groups – who simply saw Walker as a traitor for introducing the character in the first place. *Stars & Stripes*, the magazine issued by the American military, and some Southern newspapers dropped the strip – but more than 100 new newspapers picked it up. That Flap is such a stereotype is consistent with the rest of the characters in the strip, and therefore less offensive than it might seem. The fact that Walker very consciously gave him a big ego also makes it hard to find him provocative.

THEN BACK INTO
THE BLACKNESS OF
NIGHT - LIKE A PANTHER
THIS BLACK WARRIOR
DID SLIP - AND SLID
FROM THESE SHORES
AGAIN, TO THE
SAFETY OF THE
MOTHER COUNTRY
  AFRICA.
AND A DEED
WELL DONE

RIGHT ON

There were of course other cartoonists in the underground movement, besides Crumb, who used Black characters. One obscure example of this is *The Adventures of Black-eldridge the Panther*, by Ovid P. Adams. This comic tells the strange story of a Black man who, after being persecuted in the U.S.A., moves to Africa and from there raids America, avenging evil deeds inflicted upon Blacks. In the first (and only?) issue, from 1970, an owner of a shop shoots a Black man in the leg for not being able to pay for a drum he has taken a fancy to. The news of this reaches Blackeldridge, who reacts by going to America and decapitating a Mormon leader, who for some unexplained reason is pointed out as "the most responsible person." The book was printed by Marcus Books in San Francisco, with the label "Black Illustrated Drama Komics Mini Magazines co.," which indicates that it was supposed to be the first of many. The fact that neither this, nor any other comic from this publisher, has ever been mentioned in any book about underground comics indicates that it was not a resounding success.

As stated earlier, superhero comics can give the creators the opportunity to say things about our society – much in the same way as old folk tales do. Considering that the genre relies on people walking or flying around in spandex, the risk of it all becoming silly or just plain embarrassing is always present, though. Nowhere is the latter more apparent than in the story "**I Am Curious (Black)!**," which was the lead story in the comics magazine *Lois Lane* #106 from 1970. This comic was created by the trio of Robert Kanigher, Werner Roth, and Vince Colletta, and showed Lois Lane trying to understand the lives of the Black citizens of Metropolis by having Superman use Kryptonian technology to transform her into a Black person. The title's allusion to the then X-rated movie *I Am Curious (Yellow)* is rather obvious, but Kanigher has cited the 1964 movie *Black Like Me*, an adaptation of the white journalist John Howard Griffen's book about posing as a Black man in the South, as his major inspiration. Although cringe-inducing today, the story was reportedly well received in its day.

omic strips in America, and mostly in the rest of the world as well, are expected to be inoffensive. This does not apply to *Doonesbury*, by the American Garry Trudeau, however. He started drawing for various college newspapers and was signed in 1970 by the Universal Press Syndicate. Trudeau has never shied away from difficult subjects and has on several occasions been banned from newspapers for doing what no "stripmaker" should do – taking a stand. The strip started out as a story about some college friends, but has evolved and is now a complex weave of characters and relationships that have grown over thirty years. The character to the left is Calvin, or Cal for short. He was introduced – as early as 1971 – as the first recurring Black character in the strip. He was active in the Black Panthers, but was obviously deemed too one-dimensional, since he only lasted about 25 strips. There have been several other Black characters in the strip's history, though – most memorable may be Ginny, a student who, in the middle of the 1970s, ran for Congress as a seminar project.

Blaxploitation was a trend within American films during the first half of the 1970s; it was mostly action-oriented films with low budgets, geared toward entertainment rather than reflection. The major factor, though, was that they contained Black heroes and were aimed at a Black audience. The biggest hit of this genre was the film *Shaft*, from 1971 – but over sixty films were made before the audiences lost interest in this particular form of entertainment. The American comics industry soon jumped on the bandwagon and adapted this concept to its most popular genre: superheroes. Since superhero comics are aimed at younger readers than the films, the main character's sexuality (which had been a major part in the films) was toned down. *Luke Cage, Hero for Hire* was one of these "blaxploitation comics," and Cage in 1972 also became the first Black character to have his name as the title of an American comics magazine. The character was created by Stan Lee, written by Archie Goodwin, drawn by George Tuska, and inked by Billy Graham. Of all these people, only Graham is actually Black.

In the 1960s a new generation of French cartoonists was debuting, creating comics for adult readers. This was an era of great social and political upheavals in Europe, and the new comics reflected this with satire and attacks on all forms of governmental institutions. One of the most important creators in this generation was the Frenchman Jean-Marc Reiser. He debuted in 1960 in the new French magazine *Hara Kiri*, in which his aggressive drawings and brilliant observations of human weaknesses made him a role model for a whole generation of French comics creators. In the beginning of the 1970s he worked for the magazine *Pilote* and drew a number of comics making fun of our conception of native Africans. The panel to the left was taken from "**Le missionnaire**" (The Missionary), which tells the story of an overzealous preacher who stalks a native for a whole day until he relents and is christened. The preacher then adds a line on a chalkboard and celebrates with a drinking spree, offending everyone in the village. The next day he wakes up with a hangover, erases all the lines on the board, and starts afresh...

166

The years around 1970 were a period of change and, in terms of comics, a time of firsts. A man who was a vital part of this and contributed a fair share of firsts himself was the American Richard "Grass(hopper)" Green. Debuting as an artist in early 1960s fan magazines such as *Alter Ego*, *The Comicollector*, and *Komix Illustrated*, he was the first Black artist to win fame within so-called "fandom," a loosely associated group of people with a love for the comics medium. He also became the first Black to work in the underground movement, where he produced the hard-hitting magazine *Super Soul Comics* in 1972. For this magazine Green created parodies of both the superhero and detective genres, complete with Black heroes like Soul Brother American – who seemed more interested in sexual conquest than fighting his arch-enemy "Bigots, Inc." Although humorous in tone, Green's stories carried a hard-edged attack on racism and bigotry in America, so hard-edged – even for the underground movement – that the magazine never reached a second issue.

168

Nigeria was, during the 1970s, the base for the comics magazine *The Powerman Comic*, which in the context of this book is very interesting. It was published every other week starting in 1975 and was part of an attempt to create a comics culture for the African continent. Sadly, none of the cartoonists involved were from the African continent themselves; the comics were written by two Britons, Donne Avenell and Norman Worker, and drawn by two other Britons who later would become very famous: Dave Gibbons and Brian Bolland. As is often the case with such well-meaning projects (such as the TV series *Cosby*), there were *only* Black characters in these comics. The stories and drawings are more or less copies of the traditional superheroes of the time, or rather the creators' memories of the more naïve comics of the 1950s – which is notable in the simple way they divide the world in good and evil. Powerman is a slightly disguised Superman, complete with cape, a big letter on his chest, and leopardskin tights... Not surprisingly, this project did *not* jumpstart an African comic culture.

DEN DAG I APRIL
1652, DÅ DENNA
BERÄTTELSE TAR
SIN BÖRJAN, SATT
MIN FOSTERFAMILJ
OCH JAG OCH ÅT
UNDER SOLSKYDDET
I MAMMA SEWAAS
GÅRD. PLÖTSLIGT
HÖRDES EN TAL-
TRUMMA FRÅN
SKOGEN ---

Scandinavian comics were, for a very long time, almost completely devoid of Black characters. It took an even longer time before any nuanced, non-racist Black characters were presented. This is probably due to demographics; Black people were quite simply rather uncommon in most Scandinavian countries. During the wave of international solidarity that was prevalent during the 1970s, this was turned around 180 degrees, as comics creators almost tried too hard to present intelligent and noble African natives. One such comic was *Johan Vilde* (Johan the Savage), written by the Swede Janne Lundström and drawn by the Catalonian Jaime Vallvé – published in four albums between 1977 and 1982. The stories takes place in the 17th century and follow the Swedish ship's boy Johan, who travels with a trading ship to Africa, where he after a shipwreck is adopted by an African family. With its portrayal of Black people as good and white as bad, *Johan Vilde* was clearly a step forward, but the effect would probably have been even greater if the presentation had been a bit more nuanced.

As the U.S.A. continued into the 1970s, it was clearly becoming politically correct to introduce Black characters into popular culture there as well. Another example of this is "**Code Name: Gravedigger**," from *Men of War*. This magazine debuted in 1977, with scripts by David Michelinie and art by Ed Davis and Romeo Tanghal. Michelinie had a history of using Black characters, such as the Pulsar and Black Manta, but this was the first time that he got to write about a Black main character. Gravedigger was a soldier named Ulysses Hazard who enlisted in WWII, but was not allowed into battle due to racism and assigned to the graveyard detail. Realizing that the skills he'd developed were being wasted, he went AWOL and made an appeal to officials in Washington. After this he was turned into a so-called "one-man commando unit." Gravedigger went on to headline the entire 26-issue run of *Men of War* – which, considering that the basic premise of the story was racism, was remarkable. As a comment on the problems of the non-integrated American forces of WWII the story seems a bit feeble, though.

174

Westerns – on film as well as in comics – are a genre surprisingly devoid of Black characters, this despite the fact that Westerns take place in a time and location historically inhabited by Black people. The reason for the Blacks' exclusion might be that the genre represents a romanticized reality, in which racial conflict is exclusively the domain of Native Americans and white settlers. When Black characters do take major roles, the point is more often to belatedly acknowledge "the other racial conflict" than to utilize the characters as characters. The panel is from the Italian series *Tex Willer*, written by Giovanni Luigi Bonelli and drawn by Erio Nicolo. This specific story, "**In the Gallows' Shadow**," comes from 1978 and tells of a Black man's insistence on entering a whites-only saloon. Willer reluctantly arrests the Black man, who explains that "I'm only guilty of being a Negro!" The tale might have been inspired by American Black activist Rosa Parks, who in 1955 famously refused to sit in the back of a public bus – where Blacks were then required to ride – thus precipitating the historic boycott.

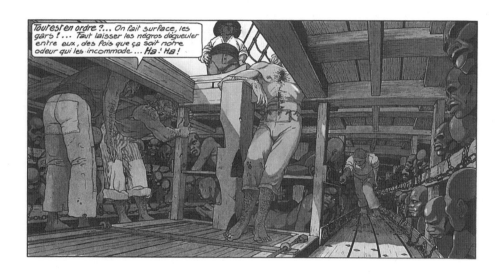

176

During the 1980s there was a trend in European comics to do adventure stories with a historical background. The comic that started this trend was *Les Passagers du vent* (Passengers of the Wind), an album series by the French comics artist François Bourgeon. The albums were published between 1979 and 1984, but the story took place in the 18th century. This epic picaresque novel is staged on various sailing ships, one of which is a slave trader sailing to the African kingdom of Juda to buy prisoners of war from the Black king. The slaves are then packed extremely tight and shipped under appalling conditions to America. Bourgeon's strengths rest in his his well-researched, and historically accurate stories, and his believable characters – who often are very strong-minded females. His world is not easily divided into good and bad, and separate characters, or whole nationalities for that matter, are never presented as either good or bad. Bourgeon's characters are human, a fact that very much includes Blacks. The immoral and inhuman aspects of slavery are also shown without the reader ever feeling that he is being lectured to.

Xenophobia, the fear of the unknown, is the theme of the series *X-Men*. The basic idea behind this comic is that some people are different because of mutations that have given them supernatural powers. A recurring theme is the fear that "ordinary" people feel for these "new" humans – often interpreted as an allegory of racial tensions. What can be ascertained is that the civil rights movement was in full swing when Stan Lee and Jack Kirby created the series in 1963. It is not unreasonable to assume that the two leaders (one who argues for coexistence and one who is a revolutionary) of the mutants were created as a parallel to the Black leaders Martin Luther King, Jr. and Malcolm X. Subsequent writers on the series have also found inspiration in the situation of Blacks in America. Despite this there was for a long time only one Black character, Storm, a female with typical European characteristics (blue eyes and long, straight white hair). In black-and-white reproduction, like this one by Dave Cockrum, Joe Rubenstein, and Bob Wiacek, from 1981, it is difficult to see that she is supposed to be Black.

180

t is not uncommon that American comics produced under license in Europe are given a rather different moral; this applies for instance to *Woody Woodpecker* comics. The Danish cartoonist Freddy Milton has written and drawn a number of comics featuring this character, who started out in animated cartoons by Walter Lantz. As in most of Milton's comics, the Carl Barks inspiration is evident – but Milton is also clearly influenced by the 1970s idea of using entertainment as a way to criticize society. In "**Rejsen til Ramashanka**" (The Trip to Ramashanka) from 1982, Woody Woodpecker works as a guide for a travelling company that arranges trips to a country inhabited by Black woodpeckers. The tourists are presented with a picturesque third world country, complete with primitive natives in grass skirts. It all turns out to be a staged reality, though, and behind it are slum districts and a travel tycoon who exploits both the natives and the prejudiced tourists. In the panel Woody, who has been painted black, says: "The turpentine is helping... I'll soon be myself again!" The native answers: "I wish we could get another color as easily..."

182

War is, or at least has been, a rather common genre in comics. Humor-based comics in this area are quite uncommon, though, probably because war is not a subject that lends itself to comedy. One exception is *Les Tuniques Bleues* (The Bluecoats), a Belgian series about the American Civil War; written by Raoul Cauvin and drawn by Willy Lambil, it actually manages to walk the thin line between humor and the horrors of war without ever becoming vulgar or coarse. This might be due to the fact that both creators are Belgian and have no emotional connections to the war in question. Black people, whose rights (at least officially) were being fought over, are most often not present in the comic. In the album "**Black Face**," from 1984, racism is the main question, though, as a Black enlisted man from the Northern army is sent to the South to stir the slaves to revolt. The main theme of this story is that the Black people on the Northern side were no better treated than the ones on the Southern side. Visually the Black characters are clearly caricatures, but then so is everybody else in this comic.

The popular notion that Islam totally forbids images is an exaggeration. In the Arabo-Islamic civilization there has been a preference for words over images, though. Arab countries *do* have comics, but they have developed late and as a reaction against imported comics from the Western world – which were seen as carrying too many Western values. Arab comics did not become a big thing until the 1970s and are mostly printed in magazines aimed at children. Due to the fact that many Arab countries have a common written language, the circulation of these can be quite high. The image is taken from the most successful and most pan-Arab of these magazines, *Mâjid* – which is published in the United Arab Emirates. One of its regular features is ***Zakiyya al-Dhakiyya*** (Zakiyya the Clever), an educational comic in which a young girl tells the readers about politics, science, history, and even religion. The panel is from the middle of the 1980s, by Ahmed Umar and Hijâzî, taken from an episode about The Ku Klux Klan, in which a marriage between a Black man and a white girl ends in the man being murdered.

186

American comics starring Archie and his friends have not exactly been noted for including ethnic characters. In the 1960s, however, the publishers did introduce Chuck Clayton, his girlfriend Nancy, and his father, coach, and gym teacher Floyd Clayton – all of whom were Black. They starred briefly in a few short stories of their own but more often appeared as supporting characters. In more recent years they have continued to appear as supporting characters, but with less and less frequency. Today both Asian and Black characters are pretty common in the background of Archie comics, giving the impression that Riverdale High is integrated, even though interracial dating, for example, has never occurred. For a while, DC had its own line of "teen" comics – such as *Binky, Date With Debbie,* and *Swing With Scooter* – and in 1971 the company introduced the three Black characters Big Sonny, Ossie, and Li'l Leroy. Sonny himself commented upon the reason for their inclusion in Keith Giffen's hilarious spoof "**Whatever Happened to Binky?**" in *Ambush Bug* #3, from 1985.

Adult comics is a term that should mean that the comics in question are aimed at thinking, adult readers. Sadly this term has more and more come to stand for erotic and/or pornographic comics. One piece of evidence out of many that it actually *is* possible to make comics for adults without sex, though, is the comic *Tales from the Heart*, a story about an American woman who signs up for volunteer work in a small village in the Central African Republic. The story, which was started in a small alternative comics magazine in 1987, is built upon the author Cindy Goff's own experiences as a volunteer. Also working on these comics were Goff's co-author Rafael Nieves and the cartoonists Seitu Hayden and Aldin Baroza. The comic deals with the main character's problems in understanding the very different culture that she meets upon arrival. Sometimes this focus can feel a bit colonial, but on the whole it is a compassionate and warm story in which the Africans are not only presented as individuals, but as equals with the white volunteers. The panel is from 1988 and drawn by Hayden.

Belgium is a country divided between two cultures based on two different languages: Dutch/Flemish and French. Belgian comics were a dominant factor in the European comics industry around the middle of the 20th century. The comics that had international success were almost only the French ones, though, and Dutch comics were mostly done for the Dutch-speaking population in Belgium and Holland. The largest success was – and is – *Suske en Wiske* (Spike and Suzy), by the Flemish comics creator Willy Vandersteen. He and his successors have, since this series was created in 1945, produced over 314 albums. The panel is from the album "**De rinoramp**" (The Rhino Disaster), from 1989; it was written and drawn by Paul Geerts and produced in association with the World Wildlife Fund. In the 1940s and 1950s the series often featured stereotypical natives, but in 1989 Black characters were represented as individuals, and as can be seen in the picture, as both good (park rangers) and bad (poachers). At the same time the main, white characters were still presented in the caricatured style of the 1940s…

192

One of the more influential American comics of the 1980s and 1990s was *Hate*, by Peter Bagge. It tells the story of the slacker Buddy Bradley, an anti-hero who just tries to get by in life. The panel is taken from the episode **"Paranoia Rules Supreme!** *or* **The Big Date Day,"** from 1991. This story is interesting because the character George (George Cecil Hamilton III) had up to this point only been presented as a person who never wanted to leave his room, or be bothered with anything except his books. The subject of his being Black had not been touched upon, and he had no distinguishable characteristics that seemed to stem from the fact that he was Black. He *is* the only major recurring Black character in *Hate*, but he doesn't give the impression of being the token Black. In this story, though, he dates a white girl (Buddy's ex-girlfriend Lisa) and becomes very aware that they are a "mixed-race couple." The date didn't work out, but that was because the weird and outgoing Lisa and the neurotic and reserved George weren't compatible as persons – not because they had different ethnic backgrounds.

Stephen Desberg is a Belgian-born American script-writer who often manages to deliver different and interesting scripts, even though he works in the field of popular culture. Together with another Belgian, Dany (Daniel Henrotin), he created *Equator* in the beginning of the 1990s. This is a two-volume album series about a white drunkard who makes a living in the middle of Africa by shipping anything in his shabby riverboat; naturally he has a heart of gold below the rugged exterior, and it is not hard to see the parallels to the Humphrey Bogart film *The African Queen*. The story in the second album deals with a dying plantation owner and his scheming offspring. That it turns out that it is the tycoon's illegitimate daughter with a native housemaid who inherits, makes me think of the novel *The Wind Done Gone* – the pastiche of *Gone with the Wind*, by Alice Randall – in which she retells the story from a slave's prespective. Even if *Equator* can be seen as yet another example of the Europeans' ambivalent relation to their colonial past, the Africans are no more of a caricature than the white people.

196

During the 1980s more and more integrated American strips started to appear in newspapers, even though it still isn't all that common today. The panel is from a 1991 Sunday page of Berkeley Breathed's *Outland*. The little girl's name is Ronald-Ann, and the whole comic was based on the idea that her life in the slum of the suburbs was so terrible that she escaped to the safety of an imaginary world, Outland. Her ethnic background was therefore probably a conscious choice, but other than that Breathed rarely seems to use this character to make statements about race. This panel, though, pokes fun at overzealous Black history makers – who sometimes have gone a bit too far when trying to establish a viable Black history. In the strip *Bloom County*, the precursor to *Outland*, Breathed introduced several Black characters, most prominently Oliver – the boy genius. Breathed sometimes used this character to comment on racial topics (often including his conservative Democrat of a father...), but mostly his place in the strip was to be the brains. Like Ronald-Ann, he doesn't feel like a "show-black."

198

Milestone Media was founded in 1992 by a group of Black American cartoonists (Derek Dingle, Dwayne McDuffie, Denys Cowan, and Michael Davis), with the aim of publishing comics with Black, Asian, and Latin American superheroes. Creating a whole new set of heroes, and not just trying to get a few more minority characters into a genre dominated by white characters, was according to McDuffie inevitable: "...my problem with writing a Black character in either the Marvel or the DC universe is that he is not a man. He is a symbol. He is all Black people." The company got a lot of criticism from Black organizations that accused them of just doing comics according to the rules set out by a white industry. The comics *were* a lot like all other superhero comics of the time, which isn't such a surprise since all the founders were seasoned professionals from this genre. Despite good intentions, the comic books from Milestone didn't sell well and today the whole line has been incorporated into DC Comics. Of all the characters, Static is the most popular, currently with a title of his own.

From South Africa comes the strip *Madam & Eve*, by the trio of Stephen Francis, Harry Dugmore, and Rico Schacherl, which deals with the life of a white housewife and her Black maid. This comic, which was started in 1992, is a sharp satire of life in South Africa after apartheid was abolished. During the time that the strip has existed, South Africa has undergone enormous changes – among which are the first free elections in 1994 – and everything has been commented upon in the strip. *Madam & Eve* is a good example of a modern comic in which Black and white characters interact on an equal basis; Eve may be the maid, but she is obviously intellectually superior to Madam. The humor of the strip often stems from people's problems in finding their roles in the "new" South Africa – as, for instance, when Madam's son comes home with his new girlfriend – who of course is Black. The strip is very popular in South Africa, and runs in both "Black" and "white" newspapers. It has even been turned into a TV series, broadcast on the national channel once known as "the white channel."

One of the largest successes of the 1990s in the American comics industry was Todd McFarlane's *Spawn*. This is an excellent example of the superhero comics of this era, which after the success of the dystopic *Batman: The Dark Knight Returns* by Frank Miller, became increasingly dark and violent. The story is centered around a man who is killed, but is given the possibility to return to his life on earth through a deal with the Devil. As in all pacts with the Devil there is a snag, and it turns out that when the main character wakes up a few years have gone by, and all that he wanted to return to has been lost. His wife has remarried and he himself has returned as a mutilated creature called Spawn. The reader also realizes, after a while, that the man was Black in his former life. It is hard to see what color his skin is in his present incarnation, but the fact remains that one of the most popular comics characters in the U.S.A. is Black. The series also deals with how he tries to relate to his former wife, her new husband, and his daughter – all of whom are Black. The panel is from 1993, drawn by Greg Capullo and McFarlane.

The three-volume album series *King* is a biography of the civil rights activist Martin Luther King, Jr. It was started in 1993, written and drawn by the Canadian Ho Che Anderson – one of the most highly-regarded Black cartoonists of North America. Anderson did not set out to make a hagiography, or, as he himself put it: "My job was not to appease whatever civil rights factions may encounter the book. My job was to tell the story as my sensibilities guided me." *King* is a graphic novel that treats Black people in a serious way, created by a Black cartoonist who clearly has the ambition to use the comics medium to communicate thoughts and ideas, and not just entertain. The result is a tough-minded book that attempts to present the man behind the myth, and in doing so it had the potential for controversy. But reaction to the book was generally positive, and it even won a Parents' Choice Award. It didn't sell as well as hoped, however (a recurring problem with Black-oriented comics), and as a result the project took a decade to finish, with the two concluding volumes appearing in 2002 and 2003, followed by a one-volume collection.

Cartoonists from Europe today have a different, if no less difficult, relationship with the treatment of Black characters, compared to their American colleagues. This is probably due to the fact that a lot of the old countries in Europe have a colonial history – something which has led to some rather apologetic comics in modern times. One example of this is the album *Zélie Nord-Sud*, from 1994, which was written and drawn by the Swiss cartoonist Cosey (Bernard Cosandey). The album tells the story of Zélie, an orphaned African girl who was adopted by a Swiss family as a child, and as a young adult returns to her home country Burkina Faso to find her roots. *Zélie* was created at the request of the Swiss DDA, which is a government organization that administers help to developing countries. That this comic was done on commission is unfortunately evident in the story, which lacks something when compared with other albums by Cosey. The story is liberating in its lack of stereotypical characters, though, as both Black and white characters are given unique features and believable personalities.

208

Even though Superman is an alien, coming from the planet Krypton, he is undeniably very "white." So when DC, Superman's American publisher, decided to kill him off and replace him with several other characters in 1993, it was a very politically correct move to have one of them be Black. The character was a construction worker named John Henry Irons, who donned a self-made iron costume and the pseudonym Steel in order to "fight for truth and justice." He debuted in *Superman: The Man of Steel* #78, but the panel is taken from the very first issue of his own title *Steel*, from 1994, by Louise Simonson, Jon Bogdanove, Chris Batista, and Rich Faber. Sharing the fate of so many other titles featuring a Black main character, it did not survive and was cancelled after 52 issues in 1998. Before its demise, the series spawned a film in 1997, written by the above-mentioned Simonson and Bogdanove and featuring Shaquille O'Neal as the main character. The quality of this movie makes you wonder if it might not have been the cause of the cancellation of the comic.

Another case of what might be seen as the result of a collective feeling of guilt over past atrocities is the Norwegian album *Kongens mann* (The King's man), from 1994, by the author Baard Enoksen and the illustrator Siri Dokken. It tells the story of Christian Hansen Ernst, an African boy who, in the early 1660s, was given as a present to a high official in the then united kingdom of Denmark and Norway and raised in the capital Copenhagen. As an adult he was given his freedom and appointed postmaster and head of customs in a small trades town in Norway – where his appearance gave the locals quite a scare. The story is based on historical facts; Ernst lived in Scandinavia between 1660 and 1694, when he was assassinated – probably by the local tradesmen who did not approve of having a Black man bossing them around. The custom of keeping "tame savages" was common in the courts of Europe in the 17th century, and the story of Ernst is just one of many sad accounts of the results of this. *Kongens mann* was published with the support of the Norwegian Antirasistisk Senter (Anti-racist Centre).

When one of the early syndicated strips that featured Blacks as main characters, *Quincy* by Ted Shearer, was ended in 1986, it was followed two years later by **Curtis**, by Ray Billingsley. Since King Features syndicated them both, one does get the feeling that the syndicate wanted to make sure they could show they had at least *one* strip with a Black character... That aside, *Curtis* has earned praise from readers, teachers, and community leaders for its contemporary humor, as well as its sensitive dramatization of serious social issues. The strip tells the story of a family living in Harlem in New York. The main character is Curtis, a normal 11-year-old boy, although his life does have a sense of inner-city perils not found in the "normal" family strips. *Curtis* is a humor strip, but treats subjects such as drug abuse, crime, and racism. Billingsley is himself Black and draws from his own childhood experiences for inspiration. The panel is from 1995. *Curtis* is still being produced, making it one of the longest running and most successful strips featuring Black characters ever.

Despite a slow but sure positive development there is still a pronounced lack of Black characters in the comics of the West. When they are presented it often seems more natural nowadays, though. Here is an example from the graphic novel *Stuck Rubber Baby*, by the American Howard Cruse, from 1995. This comic falls into the genre of social realism and tells the story of Toland Polk, a young man who grows up in the reactionary southern parts of the U.S.A. during the 1960s and discovers that he is homosexual. The story is not autobiographical, but Cruise clearly tapped into a lot of his own experiences when writing it. He addresses and weaves together the situation of the homosexuals with the growing civil rights movement of this time among the Black people of America. That Cruse wants to draw parallels between how these two groups have been treated in the U.S.A. is quite obvious. This never gets in the way of the story, though, which gives a good picture of this tumultuous era in the history of America – with protest rallies, police brutality, the Ku Klux Klan, and racism on all levels of the society.

216

Comics are still not a big thing in most African countries, even if this continent is too large and diverse to be summed up in just one statement; the Arab parts of Africa have a more lively comics culture, and comics do exist in a lot of the newspapers in South Africa. In some countries comics have been used for informational purposes, either by international organizations or by the local governments. The panel is taken from *Lishe bora kwa watoto* (Better nutrition to children), a 20-page booklet that was distributed in Tanzania through a mother and child health education program by Inades Formation-Tanzania in 1995. In addition to the story, the booklet contained specific instructions for preparing better food for children. The production of the booklet was co-sponsored by the Finnish-Tanzanian Friendship Society and the German Evangelical Centre. The writers are credited as Jane and Kitange, of whom I know very little – but the artist, Katti Ka-Batembo, is the leading campaign cartoonist in Tanzania and the founder of TAPOMA (Tanzania Popular Media Association), the cartoonists' association in Tanzania.

have deliberately not made a big thing out of the fact that some artists doing the comics cited throughout this book are themselves Black. There are other books, published and forthcoming, which deal with this subject. But sometimes it seems relevant to mention it, as with the masterful graphic novel *Nègres Jaunes* (Yellow Negroes) by the French artist Yvan Alagbé, from the year 1995. Alagbé has a French mother and a father from Benin and knows first hand what it is like to grow up with roots in two different cultures. This is also one of the themes in *Nègres Jaunes*, a beautiful combination of art and literature. Here we meet a small group of illegal immigrants from Benin, and Alagbé shows their lives without being too romantic in depicting the underdog or too eager to show the segregation of the French society. Contrasting them is a strange old man who used to be part of a special French police force comprising people from Algeria (a former colony of France) used to subdue immigrant groups. Alagbé shows with clarity and versatility how segregation and repression can take many different forms and how living in the lowest parts of society can mean different things, far from the standard clichéd image.

Despite the fact that we pride ourselves on having come a long way in fighting racism, cartoonists still seem to have a problem when treating ethnic minorities. It is inherent in comics to simplify in order to communicate, and in that process it is easy to resort to stereotypes. There are for instance still few minorities represented in Swedish comics, even though immigration has been high for several decades. One who dares to include people with other ethnic backgrounds is the comics artist Krister Petersson, who in *Uti vår hage* (In Our Meadow) even makes fun of racist thoughts. The panel is from a story from the late 1990s, in which the woman – Yvette – when meeting a Black friend on the street suddenly exclaims that she has forgotten her gingerbreads in the oven. When she arrives home she is struck with a guilty feeling that the man will have taken offense, since it was rather obvious that she associated his tone of skin with her brown cookies. Finally she goes back to apologize, but just as she arrives her appearance makes *him* exclaim that he has forgotten the Christmas ham in the oven...

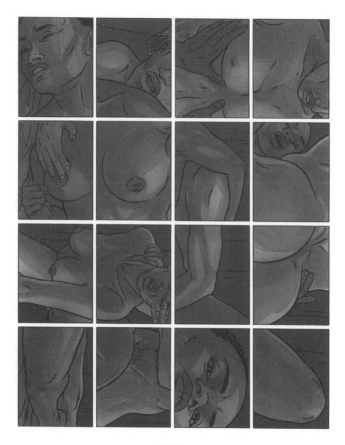

n many of the old European countries, the colonial past remains a collective guilt that needs to be addressed again and again. Like a bad itch that simply has to be scratched, there seems to be a need to tell these stories over and over again in order to come to terms with all the atrocities which were committed during the times when Europe ruled the world. These comics can be more or less realistic in their depiction of the problems of colonialism. A comic that leans towards the more realistic end of the spectrum is *Congo 40* by Éric Warnauts and Raives (pseudonym for Guy Servais), from 1996. The story is set in the Belgian Congo in the 1940s and the main character is a young Frenchman, torn between his loyalty towards the indigenous people and his inevitable connections with the white oppressors. This is shown in an allegorical way in that he is also torn among three women, a black lover and two white women, who are also mother and daughter. The main character is literally torn between the old and the new world order, and the comic does not give an easy answer as to what will be the outcome of this conflict. The scene to the left is one of the most beautiful depictions of lovemaking I have ever come across in a comic.

CARTER G. WOODSON BECAME THE FATHER OF BLACK STUDIES IN 1915 BY STARTING THE ASSOCIATION FOR THE STUDY OF NEGRO LIFE AND HISTORY.

THE HISTORY OF THE NEGRO MUST BE DOCUMENTED AND TOLD.

Combining words and pictures can have a "magical" effect, and the result is often easier to absorb and more effective than just plain texts. Comics, quite simply, have a great potential for communicating – a potential that surprisingly few seem to have discovered. Even though they are in a minority there *are* comics artists who try to create works that do more than just entertain. An interesting comic in the latter category is *Still I Rise – A Cartoon History of African-Americans*, from 1997, written by Roland Owen Laird, Jr. and Taneshia Nash Laird, and illustrated by Elihu "Adofo" Bey. This is an ambitious historical graphic novel that tries to tell the story of Black people in America – from the beginning of the 17th century up until the present day. Even though this book is thick (by comic book standards), it is of course hard to present such a large topic in about 200 pages without having to summarize heavily. Still, the creators do a good job of presenting a balanced view of the historical facts, among other things by having two "storytellers" constantly argue over the interpretation of the events.

Black characters are still rather uncommon in Japanese comics – partly because of the fear that several anti-racist campaigns have instilled in the comics community, but mostly, probably, since Black people still are almost nonexistent in the homogeneous Japanese population. When they do appear in the comics it is often hard to tell that they are Black since Japanese creators have a tendency to give all characters European features, including the Japanese. The stories that feature Blacks are often set in the U.S.A., dealing with either the police or sports such as basketball or baseball. An interesting, and critically acclaimed, story is *Eagle – The Making of an Asian-American President,* a huge, five-volume graphic novel (each volume spans over 400 pages), by the Japanese Kaiji Kawaguchi. It was started as a series in Japan in 1997 and released in the U.S.A. beginning in 2000. The story centers around an American immigrant with Japanese ancestors, who runs for the Presidency. His closest co-worker in the campaign is the man to the left, McCoy – a believable, non-stereotypical Black character.

A story that tackles the theme of Black and white in colonial France and Belgium head on is the beautifully rendered *Kid Congo* by Jacques de Loustal and Philippe Paringaux from 1997. This book garnered much praise when it was published and was awarded the prestigious Alph´Art du Meilleur Scénario (Alph´Art for best script) in Angoulême in 1998. The story follows a white woman, called Maman Rose, who falls in love with the Black man Joseph while living in Africa and takes him with her to her home in France. Since she has no money, he ends up as a prizefighter to support them, and gets the name Kid Congo. When exposed as an illegal immigrant, he is forced to join the French army at the trenches of World War I and loses a leg. As these dramatic events unfold, the relationship between "Kid Congo" and "Maman Rose" deteriorates, and in the end when she is dying, she asks that he strangles her. Joseph is throughout the story shown as stoical and gentle, and his personality is used as a contrast to the perversities of the Western world. Loustal has lived in Africa for long periods of his life, something that can be seen in his work, which often has a link to that continent.

230

As I have stated earlier, Black images in comics have not been as charged a topic in Europe as in the U.S.A. Today, with immigration to Europe at a high, there are debates on how the minorities should be integrated, but since Black people are still only a small part, the question of their representation is by no means dominant. The panel to the left is taken from the graphic novel *Jago,* by the German cartoonist Ralf König – published in 1998. The comic takes place in Elizabethan England and tells the story of Shakespeare and his actors – in an irreverent way. Since König is known for doing comics about gay characters, naturally all the actors are gay (except Shakespeare – even though the other actors do think he protests too much...). The story is loosely based on several of Shakespeare's plays, such as *Romeo and Juliet, Hamlet, Macbeth,* and *A Midsummer Night's Dream.* The misunderstood, loving couple consists of the actor Gus Philips and the huge "Moor," the latter being almost everyone's center of lustful admiration in this hilarious book.

A modern Arab comic that features not only a Black character but a female one in a leading role is *Shamsa and Dâna*, by the writer Samîra Shafîq and the illustrator Ihâb. It has been published in the magazine *Mâjid* since the 1970s and is unique in that it has two females in the leading roles – a fact that gives *Mâjid* a more pronounced female presence than any other Arab children's magazine. The girls live on an island populated by talking animals (the character in the middle is a giant pink tortoise...), and the comic has an ecological, pro-animal subtext. Shamsa is the fairer of the two and Dâna is the darker one with curly hair. In this panel, from 2000, it is evident that though Dâna still has stereotypical Black features, such as big eyes, broad lips and "kinky" hair, her skin tone is just mildly darker than Shamsa's. This has not always been so; Dâna's skin has gotten lighter over the years – even though she still is the more childish and irresponsible of the two. The fact remains, though, that this is a comic which clearly presents an image of equality, independent of ethnic background or gender.

234

The present-day American Disney company targets mothers and preschoolers more than family audiences, a state of affairs that leaves comics neglected. In Europe, however, things are quite different. Comics are still a key medium for international Disney, and older kids and adults still an important audience – much as in the heyday of the *Mickey Mouse* newspaper strip. Of course, Black characters have changed a lot since then. Blacks are still relatively rare in Disney's world, and still appear in native roles from time to time. They can, however, also be well-integrated Duckburg citizens with unquestioned authority over others. This panel is from "**Hemmelige agenter**" (Return to TNT), from 2000 – a Danish-produced *Donald Duck* story by writer Lars Jensen and artist Flemming Andersen. The character in the picture is the Head, Donald's Black boss in a paranormalist, Men-in-Black-inspired agency. "Were the *nonhuman* Astropol officers to help us," the Head says of an alien-hunting mission, "Earthlings would be panicked." Donald replies, "Snort! One Earthling is already panicked by all of this… *me*!"

A good image of France today, a France where Black people comprise a normal part of the society, is *Malika Secouss* by Tehem. This is a successful one-page humor comic, published in the magazine *Tchô!* since the late 1990s, along with, among others, the even more successful comic *Titeuf* by the Swiss artist Zep. The main character is a young Black woman living in the suburbs of a French city (probably Paris, since Tehem has lived there), hanging out with a gang consisting of two white guys and one Black guy. Malika is a kind of French version of the British comics character Tank Girl, always standing up for herself, never taking any guff from anyone, and happily kicking offending guys in the crotch with her big army boots. One favorite episode of this comic has the Black guy of the gang trying out the newly installed "Ride of Horror" at the local amusement park. To his bewilderment he gets shown a Black president of France, an interracial couple kissing, kids of all color playing together, and so on. When leaving the ride mildly confused, he finds a queue forming outside, comprising solely local skinheads…

238

Syndicates in America today still seem to hold the view that the need for diversity and equality can be satisfied by a few well-chosen comics containing Black characters. Even so, there have lately been more and more strips that challenge this old world order, and *Boondocks* by Aaron McGruder is a good example. Started as a strip in a student newspaper in 1996, it was syndicated in 1999, becoming the most successful debut ever for Universal Press Syndicate. The strip concerns two Black boys – Huey and Riley Freeman – who move from the suburbs of Chicago to live with their granddad in the very white Woodcrest. Huey is an intellectual revolutionary and Riley a "gangsta" wannabe, although the fact that both of them are less than three feet tall at times makes it hard to get people to take this seriously. Most of the strip's topics concern the relationship between white and Black people in the U.S. – mirrored through the conflicts that arise when an area "changes." In 2005 *Boondocks* was turned into a popular animated TV series, which is still running. The strip was discontinued in 2006 by McGruder himself, though, citing work on the TV series and other projects as the reason.

240

The strip *Mama's Boyz* has been running in various newspapers across the U.S. since 1990. Created by Jerry Craft, it tells the story of a single Black mother and her two sons and even though it is a traditional humorous comic strip, it has definite didactic intentions, discussing diabetes prevention, AIDS awareness, organ and tissue donation, and so on. The fact that both the creator and the characters are Black is also mirrored in the content of the comic, as can be seen for instance in the panel to the left, where one of the sons is troubled by the assignment to write about Black History Month, an annual international observance of the history of Black people in the diaspora outside of Africa. In the U.S. and in Canada, Black History Month, also called African-American History Month, is held in February. *Mama's Boyz* is something so unusual in American popular culture as a positive portrayal of an ordinary Black family, done with a lot of care and insight into family life.

A substantial part of the population of France is of African descent, having emigrated from former French colonies. Even though some are by now both second and third generation immigrants, Blacks mostly occupy the lower parts of the French society. It is therefore an interesting storytelling device to go full reverse on the assumptions this leads to and make a leading character in a comic both Black and in command of high office – with the authority and power that this entails. This is exactly the case with the album series *A.D. Grand-Rivière* by Al Coutelis and Laurent F. Bollée, of which the first volume was published in the year 2000. The main character is a commissar of the French police, and very Black indeed. The story is set in the more crime ridden outer parts of Paris, and told in a kind of tongue-in-cheek version of classical and very macho detective novels and their film-noir equivalents. This gives the writer of the series many opportunities to play with the confrontation of a strong, intelligent, and commanding Black man with the often-prejudiced French society. This comic almost reads like the old American Blaxploitation movies of the 1970s.

ealing with the repercussions of the colonial past and the role of the white man in postcolonial Africa is difficult to say the least. The 19th century style of adventure stories is no longer socially acceptable, but how do you portray white people in Africa today without being too politically correct and thereby uninteresting? Well, at least one French comics artist working today has made a name for himself by depicting Africa and the relationship between Black and white people, without using stereotypes of good or bad, of oppressor or oppressed. Jean-Philippe Stassen has made several remarkable graphic novels, of which probably *Deogratias,* from the year 2000 (published in English in 2006), is the most noteworthy. This book deals with the civil war in Rwanda, and through it Stassen actually became one of the first Western authors to publicly denounce the genocide that took place in Rwanda. In this story Stasssen uses the impossible love affair between a Tutsi and a Hutu to show the barriers of racism. The image was taken from a scene where a teacher is telling the children about the "fundamental" differences between Hutu and Tutsi.

Since the French comics culture is very much alive and exported to different parts of the world including Africa, comics influenced by the French comics are often produced in former African colonies of France. These comics rarely travel outside of Africa, though, but in the magazine *Afro-Bulles* (African bubbles, infrequently published since 2002) some can be read in French. Most comics produced in Africa are short political comics done for daily newspapers, but this magazine gives the cartoonists the possibility to tell longer stories. The comics vary from simple gags to realistic stories taken from daily life, often showing interesting differences in how ordinary everyday activities differ from life in the industrialized part of the world. The image to the left is taken from a comic by Hallain Paluku, one of these cartoonists normally working for daily newspapers, telling the ever-recurring story of how ideas are formed. The neighboring cartoonist suffering from a drought of ideas asks for an idea from the sky, and is rewarded by being hit by a falling rock, something that at least gives the first cartoonist a few ideas.

248

One of the most successful Black cartoonists of the 21st century is without a doubt Keith Knight, recipient of many awards for his work and the creator of no fewer than three popular comics and editorial cartoons: *(Th)ink* – a single panel editorial cartoon, *Knight Life* – a syndicated daily comic strip, and **The K Chronicles** – a "semiautobiographical" weekly comic strip. The panel to the left is from a strip of *The K Chronicles* from 2003 and is a parody of the popular TV series *Queer Eye for the Straight Guy*, where a group of gay designers and fashion gurus make over a straight man, his wardrobe, apartment, and so on. Knight's version, in which the five Black men invade the home of a white man, soon has a neighbor calling the police, with an ensuing shootout and the police being exonerated by a jury in the final panel, for simply doing their job. Funny and politically to the point.

250

There is a tradition of European cartoonists telling stories set in the gunslinger era of America, like *Lucky Luke, Blueberry,* or *Comanche.* These comics often contain romantic version of the Wild West, with brave gunmen, noble Indians, and beautiful women to protect. In the new wave of French comics, this image has been altered. A good example of this is the series ***Kuklos*** by Sylvain Ricard and Christophe Gaultier, started in 2003. Not only is it done in the modern, sketchy line made popular by artists like Joann Sfar and Christophe Blain, but the depiction of the "Wild West" is much dirtier and more realistic. The series is set in the early part of the 20th century and follows a young white boy brought up in the south by loyal Klansmen parents. It shows how he is socialized into the thoughts and behavior of the Ku Klux Klan: a gritty and often graphically violent story, in which the Black people are not only shown as victims, but also fight back. In a strong sequence in the first volume, the lyrics to the song *Strange Fruit,* originally sung by Billie Holiday, are contrasted with hallucinatory images of hanged Black men coming back for revenge.

Another rendezvous with the colonial past of Europe can be found in the series *La Grippe Coloniale* (Colonial Flu) by French creators Huo-Chao-Si and Apollo. The first volume was published in 2003 and tells the story of four friends returning from World War I to the French island of Réunion in the Indian Ocean. Their camaraderie goes beyond status and color, as one of them belongs to the aristocracy and one is a Senegalese Black man. The main character is a man of the people and on arrival home he is employed at the local hospital. There he is witness to the outbreak of la Grippe Espagnole (the "Spanish" flu), which was brought to the island by the homecoming soldiers and totally devastates the society, killing high and low. In the midst of this turmoil, we follow the Senegalese soldier, who despite his two awards for bravery in the war is constantly subjected to a series of small but obvious acts of discrimination. This comic is a prime example of modern French comics, combining the clear storytelling and iconic characters of *Tintin* with a realistic story that conveys thoughts and ideas about history and the society in which we live.

Sometimes a story will take on a life of its own. That is definitely the case with the story of Stagger Lee Shelton, a Black man who was convicted of murdering William "Billy" Lyons in 1895 in St. Louis, Missouri. Had this otherwise unmemorable crime not been immortalized in a song, Stagger Lee might have been forgotten. The song grew very popular, though, and has been performed and recorded by a number of artists, including the Grateful Dead and Nick Cave and the Bad Seeds. The earlier version of the songs were especially popular among Black people, and Stagger Lee soon turned into folklore: a mythical figure, a trickster and an archetype of a tough, no-nonsense Black man. In the graphic novel *Stagger Lee* (2006) by Derek McCulloch and Shepherd Hendrix, the story of Stagger Lee is told using as much factual evidence as can be found. The really interesting part of the book, though, is when the permutations of the story are examined and compared to the changing times that have influenced it. When the story traveled west, for instance, the tough guy Stagger Lee turned white…

good example of how far we have come in terms of depicting Black people in comics is the graphic novel *Nat Turner* (2008) by Black American artist Kyle Baker. This is the story of the Virginia slave rebellion in 1831, when at least 55 white slave owners and their families were killed and more than 100 slaves and free Black Americans were executed or killed by mobs in the aftermath. The leader of the uprising was the slave Nathaniel "Nat" Turner, who was convinced he had visions from God, giving him a mission to "slay my enemies with their own weapons." Turner led the rebellion with some of his fellow slaves but was finally caught, sentenced, and hanged. Baker tells this terrible story of oppression and violence with beautiful sepia images and no dialogue whatsoever. This leads you as a reader to experience the story in a much more intimate way, but it also reflects the distance between the slaves and their owners, who often did not even speak the same language.

When Barack Obama was elected, a torrent of comic book appearances by the very first Black American president ensued. One of the first was a biography in comics format, issued when he was still running for president, but the one that really got the trend started was a short backup story in *The Amazing Spider-Man* #583 (2009), by Zeb Wells, Todd Nauck, and Frank D'Amata, where Spider-Man saves Obama from an attempted assassination at his inauguration. Obama was also featured prominently on the cover, and it was made public that he was an avid Spider-Man collector as a child. This issue of *The Amazing Spider-Man* was the number-one best-selling comic book for two months in a row and ended up being the best-selling regular series comic book of the 21st century. This success started an avalanche of comic books with Obama on the cover, including such interesting (?) titles as *Barack the Barbarian* and *President Evil*. There was even a biography of the Obama family's dog, titled *Puppy Power: Bo Obama…*

He resolves upon returning home to be more like Gandhi. First thing he do is set a day aside for meditation and reflection.

YOU KNOW ABOUT HOW LONG THAT LAST.

THINGS TO DO. PEOPLE TO SEE.

KING ACCEPT THAT HE IS NOT THE MOST DISCIPLINED OF HOLYMEN.

Comics have become a truly international phenomenon, slowly blurring the once marked cultural borders between the French/Belgian, the American, and the Japanese/Asian comics cultures. A good example of this is the graphic novel *I See the Promised Land* (2010). This book was written by African-American writer, self-proclaimed griot (a West African term for storyteller), and blues singer Arthur Flowers, with art by traditional Bengali scroll-painter Manu Chitrakar and layout by Italian designer Guglielmo Rossi. This is an unorthodox biographical story of Martin Luther King, Jr. with personal, often poetic texts and colorful images from the Bengali tradition of Patua, in which a storyteller sings the story and points to images on a scroll. The publisher introduced the writer and artist to each other at a workshop, and the combination proved a fruitful one. The mix of modern visual storytelling and traditional Bengali images is eclectic to say the least and does not resemble any other comics I have ever read.

Spider-Man is one of the most popular comics characters in the world and the character behind the mask, Peter Parker, is like so many other superheroes very much a WASP. This was to change in 2010, though, when the **Spider-Man** in the alternative Ultimate Marvel Universe was killed and replaced by Miles Morales (*Ultimate Fallout* #4), a young man with a Black father and a Puerto Rican mother. The change was criticized for being too politically correct or simply done as a publicity stunt, but writer Brian Michael Bendis and artist Sara Pichelli have been creating some genuinely solid stories, showing that they have a plan for this character other than making him a token Black. According to editor-in-chief of Marvel, Axel Alonso, the idea for a Black Spider-Man came a few months before the election of Barak Obama as president of the U.S. When they realized that the very first Black American President would probably be elected, they "acknowledged that maybe it was time to take a good look at one of our icons." Opportunistic or not, it most assuredly is a sign of the times.

have tried, in the texts that accompany my visual examples, to continuously show how changes in the society are mirrored in the comics. In this epilogue, though, I would like to reflect a bit more on the trends that I have been able to discern in the material presented.

The comics that I have chosen stretch over almost two centuries – a period that has seen more radical changes than any period in the history of humankind. One trend that is easily discernable is that in the U.S.A. before the Second World War, stereotypical images of Black people were fairly common – often as minor characters. It was in this period that all the stereotypical images of toms, mammies, piccaninnies, etc. were established. They functioned as easily accessible icons that could be used by the cartoonists as storytelling tools and were expected to suggest to the reader certain associations such as servility, laziness, superstitiousness, and so on. After the Second World War these stereotypes disappeared almost totally from the comics, except in those that took place in the jungle (*The Phantom* and *Tarzan* among others) – where the stereotype of the native still was being used. After the Black characters more or less vanished from the comics it would take a long time before they were allowed to return. It quite obviously was, and still is, hard for cartoonists to treat this burning subject in a way that doesn't offend a large part of their readers. Either you annoy the ones who think you aren't progressive enough, or you annoy the ones who think you should be more conservative and cautious. You'll probably end up offending both groups. No wonder most cartoonists have avoided – and keep on avoiding – exposing themselves to this, and rather take the "safer" route of not addressing ethnic and racial questions at all. In the end it's all a question of economics, since most comics – and especially comic strips – exist within a very reactionary market, where the inclusion of a Black character can mean loss of customers. This also seems to apply to the market for comics magazines, where a Black character clearly has less chance of survival. It is probably not just a fluke that several of the most successful Black characters, such as Storm in the *X-Men* and Spawn, in reality are very hard to distinguish as being Black.

The above reasoning seems to apply mostly to the U.S.A. In Europe, the question of Black images in popular culture has not been as contentious, even if it (as I have mentioned before) is influenced by a collective bad conscience, stemming from the colonial times. The stereotypical Blacks persisted longer in European comics, but they were depictions of the native, rather than of Black people from the cartoonist's own environment. The transition to a more nuanced representation seems to have happened more quietly and without big debates and commotion.

A trend that seems common to both sides of the Atlantic is that it wasn't until the possibility of doing comics for adults became a reality that Black characters without all the stereotypical attributes started to appear. This, of course, is linked to the fact that comics for adults were a phenomenon that grew out of the 1960s movement for a more equal world and a liberal view with regards to differences between national groups. It is probably also tied in with the fact that creators working with comics aimed at an adult audience were given a chance to develop both stories and characters with more nuances. A third explanation might be that it wasn't until the boom of adult comics that the medium was being taken seriously, both by cartoonists and readers – and that this made it possible to break free from the ingrained simplifications that comics up until then had had to live with.

During the 1960s and 1970s it was, especially in the U.S.A., "hip" to raise questions of race in comics, something that the large collection of "milestones" that I have presented from this period clearly indicates. This trend seems to have gone out of vogue during the yuppie era of the 1980s, and it wasn't until the 1990s that it again became fitting to deal with Black characters, racism, integration, etc. in comics. Today there are several successful comic strips including *The Boondocks*, *Curtis*, *Madam & Eve*, and so on, that are internationally syndicated (and not just distributed to magazines specifically aimed at a Black audience). Within the more alternative comics scene there are, in the wake of comics' newfound status as a "serious art form," more and more comics that take a stand against stereotypes and present a more serious view of our complex world – where characters aren't given certain attributes solely based on their cultural background.

Referring back to the theory that I presented in the "Prologue," that racism in comics can be distinguishable on three levels, I think that the positive development when it comes to the representation in words and pictures is quite obvious, but far from complete. Blacks in comics are still sadly few, even if they – when they do appear – seem to be less stereotypical. Quite often there is the feeling that a Black character is included just to be *the* Black character in a certain context. The inclusion of people from different ethnic minorities without being representatives of their whole group is still relatively unusual. When examining the third, content-based level it is possible to distinguish a development from the judgmental attitude towards race of the era of vulgar Darwinism, to today's more liberal view of the equality of men (and women). It is of course not as simple as that, though, and even if openly racist images no longer are socially acceptable, that doesn't mean that racist prejudices have been extinguished. It would for instance have been interesting to do a special study on how different ethnic minorities are treated in comics today, which roles they are assigned, which personalities they are given, and so on.

What is probably needed are more Black cartoonists, because of the simple fact that – as numerous sociologies have reported – it is impossible to give a totally correct view of someone else's life. It should be noted, though, that it has not always been easy to determine which cartoonists are Black and which are not. That some, such as for instance the creator of *Krazy Kat*, George Herriman, spent their whole lives denying or concealing their backgrounds is sadly not all that unusual. There are numerous Black cartoonists, especially in the U.S.A., but most of them seem to do comics in the same tradition as the majority (that is to say the white part) of the cartoonists. In a way this of course is not so strange – but still a shame. Comics is an art form still in its infancy, and it will take a lot of cartoonists with different cultural backgrounds to make it grow to its full potential.

Finally, I hope that this book is the starting point of a great debate. I look forward to seeing many more books on this subject, and that you – who now have read my little contribution – feel that you in turn want to contribute by writing more thoroughly about any of the many topics that I only have had the chance to touch upon.

Quite a lot has been written about how Black characters have been treated in comics, even if these texts have been scattered over various newspapers, small parts or whole chapters in books, Internet sites, etc. I will in this section, for those of you who want to read more, present an annotated list of the texts that I have found most useful. There are, of course, many interesting books on racism, Black history, how Blacks have been treated in popular culture, etc. These I have chosen to exclude from my list to be able to focus on the texts that actually deal with Black images in comics (even among these I have only chosen the ones that I found most interesting). I have also chosen to exclude texts that were not in English, since I assume this is the language most of the readers of this book might be interested in.

For more comprehensive lists of related texts I recommend either the bibliography "Ethnicity and Cartoon Art" in the first issue of the magazine *Inks* (published by The Ohio State University), or John Bullough and Michael Rhode's incredible Internet site *Comics Research Bibliography* – where you can search on topics and click on "African-Americans" (http://www.rpi.edu/~bulloj/search/BLACK.html). I prefer shorter, but annotated bibliographic lists myself – which is what you're getting here:

Appel, John J., "**Ethnicity in Cartoon Art**" (in Cartoons and Ethnicity, The Ohio State University Libraries 1992) – An interesting article that, because it has a wider scope than my book (in cartoons the author includes all forms of drawn caricatures), goes back further in time, and examines how, and why, stereotypes work.

Brown, Jeffrey, *Black Super-heroes, Milestone Comics & Their Fans* (University Press of Mississippi 2000) – A whole book about Milestone Media, the superhero company which was owned and run by Black comics creators, and whose aim it was to introduce more characters with Black, Asian, and Hispanic backgrounds.

Canemaker, John, *Felix – The Twisted Tale of the World's Most Famous Cat* (Pantheon Books 1991) – A very thorough book about Felix the Cat, which among other things examines his inheritance from Black stereotypes, his lineage from Sambo (of *Sambo and his Funny Noises*), etc.

Carpenter, Stanford W., "**The Tarzan vs. Predator Comic Book Mini-series: An Ethnographic Analysis**" (In *International Journal of Comic Art* Vol. 1, No. 2, John A. Lent 1999) – A study of the production of an American comic book, and how the contributors, and the system in which the book is produced, affect issues of ethnic representation.

Carpenter, Stanford W., "**Alex Simmons and the African-American Soldier of Fortune Known as Blackjack: A Case Study in Independent Comic Book Publishing**" (In *International Journal of Comic Art* Vol. 4, No. 1, John A. Lent 2002) – An extensive and well-researched look into the Black cartoonist Alex Simmons' struggles to get his character Blackjack published.

Davenport, Christian, "**Black is the Color of My Comic Book Character – An Examination of Ethnic Stereotypes**" (in *Inks* vol. 4, No. 1, The Ohio State University 1997) – A thorough look at how Blacks have been treated in American superhero comics from the 1960s up until 1997. Foster III, William H., "**The Image of Blacks (African-Americans) in Underground Comix: New Liberal Agenda or Same Racist Stereotypes?**"

(In *International Journal of Comic Art* Vol. 4, No. 2, John A. Lent 2002) – An interesting subject that is sadly treated in a far too short article that focuses on but a few examples from the Underground period.

Duffy, Damian & Jennings, John, *Other Heroes: African-American Comic Book Creators, Characters and Archetypes* (Catalog for the Exhibition with the same name 2010) – An art catalog with sample pages and illustrations from a vast array of African-American comics artists, and texts by among others R. C. Harvey, Nancy Goldstein, and Bill Foster.

Duffy, Damian & Jennings, John, *Black Comix: African-American Independent Comics Art and Culture* (Mark Batty Publisher 2010) – A reworking of the earlier exhibition catalog *Other Heroes* by the same editors, with more creators represented and updated examples.

Federici, Sandra/Marchesini Reggiani, Andrea/Repetti, Massimo, *Maitite Africane: Fumetti e vignette dall'Africa* (Edizioni Lai-momo 2002) – An Italian book, collecting essays on African comics and an ample collection of sample pages, many of wichare reproduced in full color. A treasure trove of information about this sadly neglected area of comics culture.

Foster, Wiliam H., *Looking for a Face Like Mine* (Fine Tooth Press 2005) – A collection of essays and interviews about the subject of African-American creators of comics as well as the representation of African-Americans in comics.

Foster, William H., *Dreaming of a Face Like Ours* (Fine Tooth Press 2010) – The second collection of essays, articles, and interviews by the seemingly unstoppable Professor William H. Foster III, on the depiction of African-Americans in comics.

Fraser, Ben & Lindvall, Terry, **"Darker Shades of Animation – African-American Images in the Warner Bros. Cartoon"** (in *Reading the Rabbit – Explorations in Warner Bros. Animation,* Rutger University Press 1998) – I'm including this article even though it deals with animation, since many of the characters discussed – such as Felix the Cat or Bosko – were also featured in comics.

Gifford, Dennis, "**Black comics: From Li'l Mose to Black Goliath**" (in *International Book of Comics*, Optimum Books 1984) – An interesting, if rather brief, chapter within a big book by a British comics expert, who sets out to cover the whole comics history of the (Western) world.

Goldstein, Nancy, *Jackie Ormes: The First African-American Woman Cartoonist* (The University of Michigan Press 2008) – A thorough and richly illustrated biography of a fascinating cartoonist, Jackie Ormes, who managed to have a successful career in a time when Black women were given few opportunities in the U.S. A great and much needed reference work.

Gordon, Ian, "**Comic Art and the Commodification of African-American Typographies: The Limits of the Form**" (in *Comic Strips and Consumer Culture 1890-1945*, Smithsonian Institution 1998) – An interesting chapter on how Black characters in general were treated in the period that the author sets out to examine, with special focus on *Poor Li'l Mose*, *Sambo and his Funny Noises*, and *Krazy Kat*.

Groth, Gary, **"Nabile Hage. 'I will always speak out'"** (in *The Comics Journal* #160, Fantagraphics 1993) – An interview with the outspoken Nabile Hage, a Black comics scriptwriter, publisher, and member of ANIA, who grew up in Liberia but now works in America.

Hardy, Charles, **"A Brief History of Ethnicity in the Comics"** (In *Nemo – the Classic Comics Library* #28, Fantagraphics Books 1987) – Delivers exactly what the title indicates, a history of how Blacks, Jews, the Irish, Italians, Asians, etc. have been treated in American comics.

Harrington, Oliver, **"View from the Black Stairs"** (in *Inks* volume 1, No. 1, The Ohio State University 1994) – The pioneer cartoonist Oliver Harrington reminisces about his life as a Black creator in a media dominated by white editors.

Inge, M. Thomas, **"Was Krazy Kat Black? The Racial Identity of George Herriman"** (in *Inks* volume 2, No. 2, The Ohio State University 1996) – An article that examines the commonly held notion that Herriman was part Black, and how this may have influenced his career and his comics.

Jackson, Tim, "**A Salute to Pioneering Cartoonists of Colour**" (www.clstoons.com 1998-2002) – This is, as far as I know, the only thorough collection of facts about comics in the Black press of America. A treasure trove of information.

Johnson, John J., **Latin America in Caricature** (University of Texas Press 1980) – A thorough look at how South America has been portrayed in caricatures from the U.S.A. Contains the interesting chapter "The Republics as Blacks."

Jones, Steven L:, "**From 'Under Cork' To Overcoming: Black Images in The Comics**" (In *Nemo – the Classic Comics Library* #28, Fantagraphics Books 1987) – One of the best overviews of how Black characters have been treated in American comics.

Kunzle, David, "**Imperialism in Africa: Wild Beasts and Natives, Explorers and Artists**" (in *The History of the Comic Strip: The Nineteenth Century*, University of California Press 1990) – An interesting chapter in Kunzle's seminal volume on the very early history of comics.

Lee, George L., **Interesting People: Black American History Makers** (Ballantine Books 1989) – A book by and about George L. Lee, a Black cartoonist who did portraits in words and pictures of famous Black Americans. These were syndicated in daily newspapers in the U.S.A. during the 1930s and 1940s – a time when the history of the Blacks was not always treated all that well.

Maliki, Boyd/Ogowo, Ossie, "**Comics from the Old Country**" (in *The Comics Journal* #160, Fantagraphics 1993) – A (far too) short interview with two cartoonists from Nigeria about the state of the comics culture in their country.

McCloud, Scott, "**Minority Representation**" (in *Reinventing Comics*, Paradox Press 2000) – The American comics theoretician McCloud shares his thoughts on the representation of ethnic minorities in one chapter of his latest book.

McDonnell, Patrick/O'Donnell, Karen/de Havenon, Georgia Riley, *Krazy Kat: The Comic Art of George Herriman* (Abrams 1986) – The big book on George Herriman, interesting insofar as Herriman spent his whole life denying the fact that he was part Black.

Nederveen Pieterse, Jan, *White on Black: Images of Africa and Blacks in Western popular culture* (Yale University Press 1992) – A compelling illustrated history of the development of European and American stereotypes of Black people over the last two hundred years. Reproducing a wide range of intriguing images – many of which are from comics.

Nelson, Pamela B., **"From Subhuman to Superhuman: Ethnic Characters in the Comics"** (In *Nemo – the Classic Comics Library* #28, Fantagraphics Books 1987) – A historical overview of how characters of different ethnic backgrounds have been treated in American comics.

Norman, Tony, **"Ho Che Anderson – 'Being a storyteller is the most important thing in my life.' "** (in *The Comics Journal* #160, Fantagraphics 1993) – An interview with Anderson at the time of the release of the first volume of his graphic novel *King*.

Norman, Tony, **"Milestone – 'This is a beginning, not a fad.'"** (in *The Comics Journal* #160, Fantagraphics 1993) – A round-table interview with Derek Dingle, Dwayne McDuffie, Denys Cowan, and Michael Davis – the creators behind Milestone Comics.

Norman, Tony, **"Seitu Hayden – 'Stories about people, just regular people.'"** (in *The Comics Journal* #160, Fantagraphics 1993) – An interesting interview with William "Seitu" Hayden, a Black comics creator who, among other things, illustrated *Tales from the Heart.*

Norman, Tony, **"Stan Shaw – 'Comics are big enough to handle whatever the Writers and the Artists can put into them.'"** (in *The Comics Journal* #160, Fantagraphics 1993) – An interview with the outspoken Black comics creator, illustrator, and cartoonist Shaw – who, among other things, did the strip *The Alan Bland Story.*

Packalén, Leif, **"Comics in the Development of Africa"** (in *International Journal of Comic Art* Vol. 1, No. 1, John A. Lent 1999) – An interesting article in which the Finnish author states that comics in Africa of the 1990s were mainly used to communicate new ideas to the broad public.

Packalén, Leif/Odoi, Frank, *Comics with an Attitude... A Guide to the Use of Comics in Development Information* (Ministry of Foreign Affairs of Finland/Department of

International Development Cooperation 1999) – A book that presents an ongoing project to sponsor workshops in comics creation in developing countries, collects various comics from these workshops and other information-comics from developing countries, and offers advice in comics form on how to get started. An important book that is being distributed throughout the world by the activists of the nonprofit organization World Comics.

Robbins, Trina, "**Hidden Treasure – Jackie Ormes brought to Light**" (in *The Comics Journal* #160, Fantagraphics 1993) – An article by comics "herstorian" Robbins about the almost forgotten Black female pioneer Jackie Ormes.

Schodt, Fredrick L., "**Black and White Issues #2**" (in *Dreamland Japan – Writings on Modern Manga*, Stone Bridge Press 1996) – The only text that I have found concerning how Black characters have been treated in Japanese comics.

Sills, Philip, "**Illusions: Ethnicity in American Cartoon Art**" (in *Cartoons and Ethnicity*, The Ohio State University Libraries 1992) – The printed version of an exhibit held at The Ohio State University in 1992. Contains full annotations of both reference material and all the art exhibited.

Spiegelman, Art, *Comix, Essays, Graphics & Scraps – From Maus to Now to MAUS to Now* (Raw Books & Graphics, 1999) – Apart from containing interesting thoughts on how and why Spiegelman drew his masterpiece *Maus*, this book reprints some texts, such as "Little Orphan Annie's Eyeballs" and "Getting in Touch with my Inner Racist," that deal more directly with the subject of my book.

Wells, John, "**The Racial Justice Experience – Diversity in the DC Universe: 1961-1979**" (in the Internet fanzine *Fanzing* 32, http://www.fanzing.com/mag/fanzing32/feature1.shtml) – A very thorough examination of the treatment of (mostly) Black characters in magazines published by the American company DC Comics, in the stated period. Wells is the expert on DC continuity, and this article is full of interesting information.

Wells, John, "**The Racial Justice Experience – Diversity in The DC Universe: 1979-Today**" (in the Internet fanzine *Fanzing* 32, http://www.fanzing.com/mag/fanzing32/feature2.shtml) – The follow-up to the above-mentioned article, which contains longer essays on the careers of some of the more distinguished minority characters of this period. A bit disappointing coming after the brilliant first article.

Winbusch, Jeffrey, "**The New Black Age of Comics**" (in *The Comics Journal* #160, Fantagraphics 1993) – An interesting summary of the state of Black cartoonists and characters in the comics industry. Very much founded in the optimistic era that was 1993.

Worcester, Kent, "**Kyle Baker**" (in *The Comics Journal* #219, Fantagraphics 2000) – The end-all interview with one of the most successful Black American cartoonists – who among other things created the graphic novel *Why I Hate Saturn*.

INDEX

A

A.D. Grand Rivière 243
Adams, Neal 155
Adams, Ovid P. 157
Adventures of Blackeldridge the Panther, The 157
Adventures of Spirou & Fantasio 11`
African Queen, The 195
Afro-American Continental Features Syndicate 117
Afro-Bulles 247
Alagbé, Ivan 219
All-Negro Comics 6
Allen, Woody 141
Ally Sloper 47
Alonso, Axel 263
Alphonse, Gaston and Their Friend Leon 57
Alter Ego 167
Amazing Spider-Man, The 259
Ambush Bug 187
Andersen, Flemming 235
Anderson, Ho Che 205
Andréassson, Rune 125
Angelfood McSpade 13, 141

Antirasistisk Senter 211
Apollo 253
Archie comics 187
Arndt, Walter 49
Association to Stop Racism against Blacks 45
Avenell, Donne 169
Aventuras del Negro Raul, Las 63

B

B.C. 15
Bachus, Joan 135
Bagge, Peter 193
Baker, Kyle 257
Bamboozled 14
Bamse 125
Barbera, Joe 105
Barks, Carl 109
Baroza, Aldin 189
Batista, Chris 209
Batman - The Dark Knight Returns 203
Bendis, Brian Michael 263
Beetle Bailey 155
Bey, Alihu "Adofo" 225

Biffen och Bananen 113
Billingsley, Ray 16, 213
Binky 187
Birth of a Nation 8
Black Comic Book, The 149
Black Face 183
Black Illustrated Drama Komics
     Mini Magazines co. 157
Black Like Me 159
Black Panther 137
Black Panther party 137, 161
Blanc, Mel 97
blaxploitation 163
Blondie 149
Blondin et Cirage 115
Bloom County 197
Bonelli, Luigi Giovanni 175
Blueberry 251
Bogart, Humphrey 195
Bogdanove, John 209
Bolland, Brian 165
Bollée, Laurent F. 243
Boondocks, The 239, 270
Bosko 81
Bourgeon, François 177

Brandon, Barbara 7
Brandon, Brumsic 7
Branner, Martin 89
Breathed, Berkeley 197
Brown, Bertie 91
Bullough, John 274
Bumbazine and Albert 99
Burroughs, Edgar Rice 101
Busch, Wilhelm 49
Buster Brown 53
Butterfly 91

C
Camileff 51
Captain America 9
Captain and the Kids 69
Captain Easy 151
Capullo, Greg 203
Cauvin, Raoul 183
Cave, Nick 255
Century of Women Cartoonists, A 7
Chittakar, Manu 261
Civilisons l'Afrique! 51
Clansman, The 8
Classics Illustrated 135

Cockrum, Dave 179
Code Name: Gravedigger 173
Colletta, Vince 159
Colón, Ernie 149
Comanche 251
Comicollector, The 167
Comics Code Authority 119
Congo 40 223
Corne du Rhinocéros, La 121
Cosandey, Bernard 207
Cosby, Bill 143, 1691
Cosey 207
Coutelis, Al 243
Cowan, Denys 199
Craft, Jerry 237
Crumb, Robert 141
Cruse, Howard 215
Curtis 16, 213, 270

D
D'Amata, Frank 259
Daly, John 103
Dany 195
Date With Debbie 187
Dateline: Danger! 143

Davis, Ed 173
Davis, Michael 199
Davis, Phil 83
DC Comics 199
de Loustal, Jacques 229
Dell Comics 95, 109
Deogratias 245
Desberg, Stephen 195
Dick Tracy 15
Dingle, Derek 199
Dirks, Rudolph 69
Disney, Walt 75, 111, 235
Dokken, Siri 211
Donald Duck 111, 235
Doonesbury 161
Dugmore, Harry 201
Duval, Marie 47

E
*Eagle — The Making of an Asian-
    American President* 227
EC Comics 119
Eisenberg, Harvey 105
Eisner, Will 93
El Hogar 63

Enoksen, Baard 211
Entertaining Comics 119
Equator 195
Evil Eye, The 127

F
Faber, Rich 209
Falk, Lee 83, 87
Fantastic Four 135
Far Side, The 16
Feelings, Tom 123, 135
Feldstein, Al 119
Felix the Cat 65, 75
Finnish-Tanzanian Friendship
      Society 217
Fipps der Affe 49
Flash, The 133
Folket i Bild 113
Foster, William H. III 23
Four Color 109
Fox, Gardner 133
Francis, Stephen 201
Franquin, André 121
Friday Foster 151
Fyrtaarnet og Bivognen 67

G
Gaines, William M. 119
Garland, Jan-Erik 113
Gasoline Alley 79
Gaultier, Christophe 251
Geerts, Paul 191
Genius of Wilhelm Busch, The 49
German Evangelical Centre 217
Gibbons, Dave 169
Giffen, Keith 187
Giordano, Dick 153
Goff, Cindy 189
Golden Legacy 123, 135
Gone With the Wind 12
Goodwin, Archie 163
Gormley, Dan 97
Graham, Billy 163
Grateful Dead, The 255
Gravedigger 177
Green Lantern/Green Arrow 153
Green, Richard 167
Greene, Sid 133
Greg 121
Grier, Pam 151
Griffith, D.W. 8

Grippe Coloniale, La 253

H
Habibu 125
Hairbreadth Harry 73
Hamlet 231
Hanna, William 105
Happy Hooligan 57
Hara Kiri 165
Harman, Hugh 81
Harriet Tubman, the Moses of Her People 135
Harrington, Ollie 8
Harris, Joel Chandler 12
Hart, Johnny 15
Hate 193
Hayden, Seitu 189
Hearst, William Randolph 69
Hemmelige agenter 235
Hendrix, Shepherd 255
Hep 7
Hergé 77
Herr Tupp 107
Herriman, George 55, 272

Hijâzî 185
Hine, H. G. 45
Hogarth, Burne 101
Huckleberry Volunteers 53
Huo-Chao-Si 253

I
I Am Curious (Black)! 159
I See the Promised Land 261
I Spy 143
Ihâb 233
Image of the Black in Western Art, The 7
In the Gallows' Shadow 175
Inades Formation-Tanzania 217
Incredible Science Fiction 119
Ising, Rudy 81

J
Jack B. Quick 17
Jacobson, Sid 149
Jago 231
James Bond 151
Jensen, Lars 235
Joe Palooka 151

Johan Vilde 171
Johnson, Jack 129
Jolly Antics of Smiler and Smudge,
    The Comical Couple of Car-
    raway College, The 91
Judge 61
Judgement Day 119
Judy, or the London Serio-Comic
    Journal 47
Jungle Action 137
Justice League of America 133

K

K Chronicles, The 249
Ka-Batembo, Katti 2179
Kahles, C. W. 73
Kanigher, Bob 129, 159
Katzenjammer Kids 49, 69
Kawaguchi, Kaiji 227
Kelly, Walt 95, 99
Kid Congo 229
Kimba the White Lion 111
King 205
King Features Syndicate 147, 213
King, Frank 79

King Jr., Martin Luther 131,
    179, 205
Kirby, Jack 137, 179
Knerr, Harold 69
Knight, Keith 249
Knight Life 249
Komix Illustrated 167
Kongens mann 211
König, Ralf 231
Krazy Kat 55, 65, 272
Ku Klux Klan 185
Kubert, Joe 129
Kuckeliku och Hilda i skolan 101
Kuklos 251

L

Laird, Jr., Roland Owen 225
Laird, Taneshia Nash 225
Lambil, Willy 183
Lanteri, Arturo 63
Lantz, Walter 97, 181
Lariar, Lawrence 12
Larson, Gary 16
Lawrence, Jim 151
Lee, Stan 137, 163, 179

Lee, Spike 10, 14
Li'l Abner 149
Li'l Eight Ball 97
L'Image pour Rire 51
Lion King, The 111
Lishe bora kwa watoto 217
Little Nemo in Slumberland 59
Lois Lane 1591
Longarón, Jorge 151
*Looney Tunes and Merrie Melodies
    Comics* 95
Lucky Luke 251
Luke Cage, Hero for Hire 163
Lundström, Janne 171
Luther 7

M

M C Squared 7
Macbeth 231
Madam & Eve 201, 270
Madsen, Harald 67
Mâjid 185, 233
Malcolm X 179
Malika Secouss 237
Mama's Boyz 237
Man In The Moon 45

Man, Thy Name Is — Brother! 133
Mandrake the Magician 10, 85, 87
Marriner, William 621, 65
Marvel Comics 199
McCay, Winsor 59
McClarty, Doris 7
McCulloch, Derek 255
McDuffie, Dwayne 199
McFarlane, Todd 203
McGruder, Aaron 239
McWilliams, Alden 143
Men of War 173
Messmer, Otto 65
MGM 81, 105
Michelinie, David 173
Mickey Mouse 65, 75
Midsummer Night's Dream, A 231
Milestone Media 199
Miller, Frank 203
Milton, Freddy 181
Minute Movies 85
missionnaire, Le 165
Mitchell, Margaret 296
Moon Mullins 71
Moore, Alan 17

Moore, Ray 87
Musical Mose 55

N

Nat Turner 257
Nauck, Todd 259
Nègres Jaunes, Les 219
Negro Americans: The Early Years 135
New Funnies 97
New York Age 123
Nicolo, Erio 175
Nieves, Rafael 189
Nowlan, Kevin 17

O

O'Neil, Dennis 153
O'Neal, Shaquille 209
Obama, Barack 259, 263
Opper, Frederick Burr 57
Orlando, Joe 119
Ormes, Jackie 117
Our Army At War 129
Our Gang Comics 99, 105
Outcault, Richard F. 53
Outland 197

P

Palaku, Hallain 247
Paringaux, Philippe 229
Parks, Rosa 175
Passagers du Vent, Les 177
Pat, Patsy and Pete 95
Peanuts 129, 139, 149
Persson, Erik 107
Petersson, Krister 221
Phantom, The 39, 87, 101, 267
Phoenix 145
Pichelli, Sara 263
Piët, Frans 89
Pilote 165
Planet Plans 85
Pogo 99
Poor Li'l Mose 53
Posro Komics 6
Powerman Comic, The 169
Puppy Power Bo Obama 259

Q

Queer Eye for the Straight Guy 249
Quincy 15, 147, 213

R

Raives 223

Randall, Alice 195
Red Sea Sharks, The 77
Regnier, Michel 121
Reiser, Jean-Marc 165
Rejsen til Ramashanka 181
Remarks on the Methods of procuring slaves 43
Remi, Georges 71
Return to TNT 235
Rhodes, Michael 274
Ricard, Sylvain 251
Roba, Jean 121
Robbins, Trina 7
Røgind, Carl 67
Romeo and Juliet 231
Ross, Charles Henry 47
Rossi, Guglielmo 261
Roth, Werner 159
Rubenstein, Joe 179

S

Sambo and His Funny Noises 6, 61, 65
Saunders, Allen 143
Schacherl, Rico 201
Schenstrøm, Carl 67

Schiff, Jack 103
Schulz, Charles M. 131, 139, 155
Sekowsky, Mike 133
Servais, Guy 223
Shafîq, Samîra 233
Shaft 163
Shakespeare, William 231
Shamsa and Dâna 233
Shearer, Ted 15, 147, 213
Shelton, Stagger Lee 255
Silence On Tourne! 115
Simonson, Louise 209
Sinnott, Joe 137
Sjors en Sjimmie 91
Sloper In Savage Africa 47
Smiler and Smudge 91
Smith, Albert 45
Smith, Win 75, 81, 95
Smurfs, The 121
Spawn 203, 268
Spider-Man 263
Spike & Suzy 191
Spirit, The 8, 95
Spirou et Fantasio 121
Stagger Lee 255

Stars & Stripes 155
Stassen, Philippe 245
Static 199
Steel 209
*Still I Rise - A Cartoon History of
    African-Americans* 225
Storm 179, 268
Stowe, Harriet Beecher 8, 35
Strange Brew 117
Stuck Rubber Baby 215
Sullivan, Pat 61, 65
Super Soul Comics 167
Superman 149, 209
Superman: The Man of Steel 209
*Surprising Adventures of Mr
    Touchango Jones, The* 45
Suske en Wiske 1913
Swing With Scooter 187

T
T. C. McClure Newspaper
    Syndicate 61
Tales from the Heart 189
Tanghal, Romeo 173
Tank Girl 237
Tarzan 101, 267

Teddy 117
Tehem 237
Tembo Tabou 121
Tex Willer 175
Tezuka, Osamu 111, 145
(Th)ink 249
Tintin in the Congo 77
Titeuf 237
Tom and Jerry 105
Tom Poes 127
Tommy Traveller 133
Toonder, Marten 127
Toppens Väv 107
Torchy Brown 117
Trudeau, Garry 161
Tuniques Bleues, Les 183
Turner, Morrie 15, 131, 147
Tuska, George 163

U
Umar, Ahmed 185
Uncle Tom's Cabin 8, 35
Universal Press Syndicate 161, 270
Uti vår hage 221

V

Vallvé, Jaime 171
Vandersteen, Willy 191
"Voodoo Hoodoo" 109

W

Walker, Mort 155
Ware, Chris 22
Warnauts, Éric 223
Warner Brothers 81
Wee Pals 15, 131, 147
Weird Fantasy 119
Wells, Zeb 259
Wersén, Gunnar 107
Whatever Happened to Binky? 187
What's the Color of Your Blood? 129
Wheelan, Ed 85
Where I'm Coming From 7
Wiacek, Bob 179
Willard, Frank 71
Wind Done Gone, The 195
Winnie Winkle 89
Woody Woodpecker 181
Worker, Norman 169
World's Finest 103

X

X-Men 179, 268

Y

Yellow Claw 9
Yellow Kid 53
Young Allies 9

Z

Zakiyya al-Dhakiyya 85
Zélie Nord-Sud 207
Zep 237

COPYRIGHTS